What If My...

pulls...won't e... ...rks...
is aggressive...jumps up...is shaking...
pees in the house...etc...etc?

Expert answers to all those doggy problems

Jim Evans

Interpet Publishing

Published by Interpet Publishing,
Vincent Lane,
Dorking,
Surrey RH4 3YX,
England

ISBN-10 1-84286-116-6
ISBN-13 978-184286-116 5

Credits
Editor: Philip de Ste. Croix
Designer: Philip Clucas MSIAD
Cartoons: Russell Jones
Diagram artwork: Martin Reed
Production management:
    Consortium, Suffolk

Printed and bound in China

This book sets out to explain how to deal with a variety of problems that a dog owner may experience in the course of everyday life. It gives advice on various measures that can be used to remedy bad behaviour, mishaps and accidents around the home and outdoors, and health problems of many kinds. Used sensibly, the suggestions contained in this book are quite safe, but readers must be aware that some dogs are strong animals that may on occasions behave unpredictably. Dogs that display characteristics such as aggression should always be approached with caution; if in doubt, seek the advice of a qualified animal behaviourist or veterinary surgeon.

The information and recommendations in this book are given without any guarantees on behalf of the author and publisher, who disclaim any liability with the use of this material.

About the Author

Jim Evans is an internationally respected veterinary surgeon, a developer of many widely used medicines and pet-care products, and a world-renowned writer and lecturer on veterinary and animal-care topics. His other published works include *Doglopaedia, Puppylopaedia, The Book of the Bitch* and *Breeding A Litter.*

Acknowledgements

My grateful thanks go to all those who have encouraged and helped me to write this book, and particularly the editorial and production team who put it together. Worthy of special mention is Kevin Kingham of Interpet Publishing, whose ideas in respect of content and presentation fired the enthusiasm of everyone who has subsequently become involved – a real entrepreneur!

I feel I must acknowledge the American Veterinary Surgeon, Vicky Voith, who was a pioneer in respect of dog behaviour and who first stimulated my interest in the subject more than 25 years ago. By no means least, I have also to express my gratitude to my wife Monica for her continuing support and constructive criticism through the trials and tribulations of authorship, I realize only too well how traumatic that can be for her and certainly no easy undertaking.

Finally very many thanks to all those people, teachers and academics especially, who have helped me throughout my career, to learn, understand and contribute a little to our present day knowledge about the causes, treatment and prevention of diseases in dogs. I am grateful also to all those veterinary surgeons, breeders, dog owners and other writers who have made it possible for me to crystallize my ideas about the intricacies of dog ownership and to put them on paper in, hopefully, an understandable and helpful way.

Dedication
To Anna the Dobermann, the original Ideal Dog,
and to *all* good dogs.

CONTENTS

UNDERSTANDING DOG BEHAVIOUR AND HOW IT CAN BE SHAPED Pages 10-49

WHAT IFs...?

What if my dog...

1 barks excessively? Page 29

2 bites and nips at people's hands and ankles? Page 29

3 chews favourite family items? Page 29

4 is aggressive towards people, strangers and possibly family members? Page 30

5 shows hypersexual traits? Page 30

6 is jealous of another dog that I own? Page 31

7 jumps up at people? Page 31

8 chases people (especially those on bicycles) and animals? Page 32

9 is overly submissive? Page 32

10 is aggressive to other dogs? Page 33

11 is disobedient and won't come when called? Page 33

12 suffers from car sickness? Page 34

13 eats its own faeces or those of other animals? Page 34

14 is too dominant? Page 35

15 suffers from separation anxiety and is over-anxious and destructive when left alone in the house or car? Page 36

16 pulls on the lead? Page 37

17 is shy with other people? Page 38

18 licks people's hands excessively? Page 38

19 begs for food or attention? Page 38

20 is possessive over food? Page 39

21 is inclined to steal food? Page 39

22 is not fully house-trained? Page 40

23 resents being groomed? Page 42

24 has a phobia? Page 43

PART 2

MISHAPS AND PROBLEMS ABOUT THE HOUSE AND OUTDOORS Pages 50-87

WHAT IFs...?

What if my dog...

25 soils my carpets or upholstery either by accident or as a result of illness? Page 52

26 has picked up oil or tar on its coat or paws? Page 54

27 is not fully house-trained and has accidents overnight? Page 55

28 territory marks by urinating against objects in the house? Page 56

29 sheds hair on the furniture, clothing or car upholstery? Page 57

30 needs to be bathed? Page 58

31 needs to be introduced to a new puppy, a new baby, or to a kitten or resident adult cat? Page 59

32 chews chair legs and doors, cushions, shoes and other commonly used items? Page 62

33 will not allow itself to be thoroughly groomed and its ears, eyes, mouth and private parts to be touched and examined? Page 63

34 will not take tablets? Page 64

35 is going to be involved in Christmas celebrations or other festive occasions – what precautions should be taken? Page 65

36 is burnt or scalded accidentally in the kitchen? Page 66

37 seems to be lonely, should I get another dog to keep it company? Page 66

38 has eaten a box of chocolates or a chocolate bar? Page 68

39 has swallowed some human medicines or tablets? Page 68

CONTENTS

40 is found unconscious by a source of electricity? Page 69

41 needs to be fed differently because of my changed circumstances – what should it be given and how many daily meals will it need? Page 70

42 is in season and there are male dogs in the house? Page 71

43 makes blood stains on the carpets and furniture when she is on heat? Page 72

44 bites visitors' hands with its very sharp teeth? Page 72

45 licks people's hands and faces? Page 72

46 objects to wearing a collar and fights the lead? Page 73

47 passes faeces on the pavement? Page 74

48 kills shrubs by urinating against them? Page 74

49 will not swim? Page 75

50 swallows a stone? Page 75

51 digs in the garden? Page 76

52 passes faeces in the garden – how are they best disposed of? Page 76

53 is stolen? Page 77

54 gets lost and can't find its way home? Page 78

55 gets into a fight with another dog? Page 79

56 is involved in a road traffic accident? Page 81

57 is caught in barbed wire or a thorn hedge? Page 82

58 picks up stones and sand on the beach? Page 82

59 does not behave well in kennels? Page 83

60 is stung by a bee or wasp? Page 83

61 is found unconscious in my car? Page 84

62 makes bleached circles on the lawn where she urinates? Page 84

63 is mated while out on a walk? Page 84

PART 3

PREVENTING AND COPING WITH ILLNESS Pages 88-147

WHAT IFs...?

What if my dog...

64 eats grass? Page 102

65 vomits? Page 102

66 refuses to eat? Page 104

67 is in danger of becoming obese? Page 104

68 is eating well but remains very thin? Page 108

69 is drinking excessively? Page 108

70 sneezes? Page 109

71 has runny eyes? Page 109

72 has eyes that look abnormal? Page 110

73 is blind? Page 112

74 is shaking or scratching its ears? Page 112

75 is holding its head on one side? Page 114

76 is breathing abnormally? Page 114

77 is shedding hair? Page 116

78 is scratching excessively? Page 117

79 keeps breaking wind? Page 120

80 is biting its tail, scooting or rubbing its bottom on the ground? Page 121

81 has diarrhoea? Page 122

82 is passing blood in its faeces? Page 123

83 is constipated? Page 123

84 is not passing urine? Page 124

85 is incontinent? Page 124

86 is passing blood in its urine? Page 125

87 has a discharge from its penis or vulva? Page 126

88 is pot-bellied? Page 126

89 is limping? Page 128

90 is coughing? Page 129

91 is eating with difficulty? Page 130

92 has bad breath? Page 130

93 is having fits, convulsions or is twitching? Page 132

94 has a lump or swelling? Page 133

95 is wounded, grazed, cut, burnt or scalded? Page 134

CONTENTS

96 is licking itself excessively? Page 136

97 is weak and lethargic? Page 136

98 has collapsed and is comatose? Page 136

99 is not breathing? Page 137

100 appears deaf? Page 138

101 is salivating excessively? Page 138

102 is over-sexed? Page 138

103 is drinking excessively? Page 140

104 is going bald? Page 140

105 is passing urine more frequently? Page 140

106 is incontinent? Page 141

107 is passing blood-stained, smelly urine with difficulty? Page 141

108 is pot-bellied? Page 141

109 has a lump or swelling? Page 142

110 is licking her vulva excessively? Page 142

111 has a vaginal discharge? Page 143

112 is mated by accident? Page 143

113 is found to be pregnant unexpectedly? Page 144

114 has signs of abdominal pain? Page 144

115 is a problem when on heat? Page 144

PART 4

THE AGEING DOG – MAINTAINING QUALITY OF LIFE IN OLD AGE Pages 148-153

WHAT IFs...?

What if my dog...

116 should become senile? Page 151

117 is becoming deaf? Page 151

118 is losing its sight? Page 151

119 is becoming incontinent? Page 152

120 has digestive problems? Page 152

121 appears to be suffering from arthritis? Page 152

122 becomes very ill and has a reduced quality of life? Should I consider having it put to sleep (euthanasia)? Page 153

Introduction

In writing this book my main aim is to try to help every dog owner to obtain all the benefits that dog ownership can bring with the minimum of hassle and worry. If the advice given is followed, you should end up the proud owner of a fun-loving dog which is sound, healthy and without any behavioural 'hang-ups'. Your dog should fit comfortably into today's society without causing you any embarrassment or friction. What's more you and your dog should enjoy reaching that goal together.

The book is divided into four parts that deal with dog behaviour, problems and mishaps about the house and outside, coping with and preventing illness and, finally, caring for dogs in old age. In each case detailed background information is given first and this is followed by sections dealing with specific problems that are commonly experienced. These problems are noted under the heading 'What if my dog...?'. Because prevention is essentially so much better than attempted cure, advice as to how to prevent and avoid possible problems occurring in the first place is also given at the end of each part.

The **'What ifs...?'** in each section of the book are designed principally to be used as a 'service manual'. Hopefully the clear layout and extensive cross-referencing and indexing will allow information on any problem that you may experience to be simply and quickly retrieved when needed.

I sincerely hope that every reader will find something of interest and assistance in the book and be encouraged to help me achieve my aim. My hope is that you will get as much pleasure from your dog as I have had with those that I have been privileged to own.

Jim Evans

UNDERSTANDING DOG BEHAVIOUR AND HOW IT CAN BE SHAPED

PART 1

CONTENTS

- **INTRODUCTION** Page 12
- **THE LANGUAGE OF DOGS** Page 13
- **HOW DOGS LEARN** Page 16
- **STAGES IN A PUPPY'S DEVELOPMENT** Page 22
- **TEACHING AIDS – TOOLS TO SHAPE BEHAVIOUR** Page 22
- **REINFORCEMENT – ESTABLISHING AND MAINTAINING A LEARNED BEHAVIOUR** Page 26
- **DOMINANCE AND SUBMISSIVENESS** Page 26
- **CONCLUSION** Page 27
- **SOLVING COMMON BEHAVIOURAL PROBLEMS** Page 28

WHAT IFs...?

What if my dog...

1 barks excessively? Page 29
2 bites and nips at people's hands and ankles? Page 29
3 chews favourite family items? Page 29
4 is aggressive towards people, strangers and possibly family members? Page 30
5 shows hypersexual traits? Page 30
6 is jealous of another dog that I own? Page 31
7 jumps up at people? Page 31

8 chases people (especially those on bicycles) and animals? Page 32

9 is overly submissive? Page 32

10 is aggressive to other dogs? Page 33

11 is disobedient and won't come when called? Page 33

12 suffers from car sickness? Page 34

13 eats its own faeces or those of other animals? Page 34

14 is too dominant? Page 35

15 suffers from separation anxiety and is over-anxious and destructive when left alone in the house or car? Page 36

16 pulls on the lead? Page 37

17 is shy with other people? Page 38

18 licks people's hands excessively? Page 38

19 begs for food or attention? Page 38

20 is possessive over food? Page 39

21 is inclined to steal food? Page 39

22 is not fully house-trained? Page 40

23 resents being groomed? Page 42

24 has a phobia? Page 43

- **PREVENTING INAPPROPRIATE BEHAVIOUR** Page 46
- **HELPFUL HINTS – DO'S AND DON'T'S** Page 48
- **SEEKING ADDITIONAL HELP** Page 49

INTRODUCTION

There is no doubt that owning a dog can be very rewarding and bring many significant benefits to owners and their families. If all goes well, having a dog as a pet will be fun and enjoyable both for the owner and the dog. However, even in the best of situations problems can arise, either because the dog was not socialized and habituated properly during the first critical formative weeks of its life, or because the methods used were not applied correctly and consistently by everyone in contact with the dog. Problems may also, of course, arise in older and adopted dogs where inappropriate behaviours have become established and deeply rooted, frequently as a result of misapplied or incorrect training. Indeed, owners are often unaware of, or will not accept, the fact that their pet does have a behaviour problem. Many people are under the false impression that some problem behaviours are simply part and parcel of dog ownership.

It is a sad fact that more dogs are now destroyed each year as a result of inappropriate behaviour than die of infectious disease. There is no need for this situation to continue. If the advice given here is heeded, the difficulties which may be met through your dog's life can usually be overcome or prevented.

A well-behaved and properly socialized dog adds an extra dimension to family life. However, problems can – and do – occur and the upshot then may be domestic discord. This book aims to help you identify why such problems arise, and to advise you on how to overcome them or, better still, prevent them.

HELPING TO OVERCOME PROBLEMS

In this section of the book the ways in which dogs think and learn are examined and the methods that can be applied to shape their behaviour outlined. Armed with this knowledge, it will be possible in many cases for you to identify the possible cause(s) of any problem and to work out for yourself how the difficulty can be overcome. Some of the more common behaviour problems are examined in detail under the heading 'What if my dog...?' and guidance is given on how owners can best cope with such situations. Importantly too, attention is drawn to those circumstances where it is vital to seek expert help either from a vet or a trained animal behaviourist.

Finally guidance is given on how undesirable behaviour problems can be avoided; prevention is generally far better than attempted cure, and that is particularly true in respect of the potentially more disruptive or dangerous behaviours.

They can't talk to us,
but they can understand us.

THE LANGUAGE OF DOGS

Because dogs can neither talk nor truly understand the spoken word, they cannot be taught right from wrong (as we can) by learning from other people's experiences. Furthermore, dogs cannot ask the all important questions, 'what?', 'when?', 'why?' and 'how?' If only dogs could ask 'Have I responded as you want?', 'Why are you cross with me?' or 'What have I done wrong?', there is no doubt that teaching and training dogs would be a doddle!

I THINK I'LL GO DOWN THE PUB.

Don't be surprised if your dog sometimes seems able to read your mind! They are very adept at interpreting our body language.

Although dogs are not able to talk, they do communicate by a quite sophisticated method – by 'body language'. As a result, dogs have become *very* astute observers. They can detect minute changes in the attitude of humans, and thus they often appear to be 'reading' their owner's mind and to be able to anticipate correctly what is about to happen. From a behavioural point of view the significance of this is that if we are to 'understand' dogs we must be able to 'read' and interpret *their* body language and use *our* adaptation of their body language, *together with* words, when we teach them how we would like them to behave. The value of using gestures *and* words is often underestimated and is certainly far more effective than shouting!

13

This posture is playful – the facial expression is eager and the tail probably wagging.

One other important implication of this fact is that we can, often quite unintentionally, encourage or 'reinforce' a dog's behaviour by an inadvertent word or gesture that the dog interprets as praise. Certainly many inappropriate behaviours in dogs stem from this cause. If the action or gesture is stopped and never repeated again, the unwanted behaviour will usually quite promptly extinguish itself and be forgotten by the dog and completely erased from its repertoire.

A dog's emotions and intentions can be read by observing its stance, how it holds its ears and tail and its facial expression. It pays to observe your pet closely as a puppy and throughout its life so that you can interpret what it is 'saying' to you. Some of the more common signs are explained in the table below.

INTERPRETING A DOG'S BODY LANGUAGE

Sign / Posture	Interpretation
Ears: Pricked/erect pointing forward	Dog alert and listening – 'I'm interested, what do you want?'
Held back to head	Submission, pleasure or ready to attack – 'Take care!'
Flat back or low on head	Fear – 'I'm sorry, don't punish me!'
Eyes: Narrowed and half closed	Pleasure or submission – 'You may approach!'
Wide open and staring	Threatening – 'I'm the boss, don't challenge me!'
Soft-eyed sideways glance	Approval – 'I like your style!'
Mouth: One-sided grin	A friendly greeting – 'You can come closer!'
Both lips pulled back to expose teeth	The start of aggression – 'Look out!'
Head lowered not barking	'I'm about to mount an attack – advance at your peril!'
Body: Standing on toes Chest thrust forward Hair on neck and along back erect	Aggression – 'I mean business!'

Aggressive stance and barking with mouth open	'I'm not sure about you and I'm rather afraid and thinking about running away – best ignore me!'
Lying on back and possibly passing dribbles of urine	'I give in – please don't hurt me!'
Tail: Carried at 45 degrees or more higher than spine	'I'm alert and interested'
Clamped down over bottom	'I'm rather nervous and afraid'
Between legs and hind quarters crouched	'I'm really nervous and afraid'
Tail gently waving	'I'm getting annoyed and thinking about being aggressive'
Tail wagging	'I'm happy and enjoying myself'

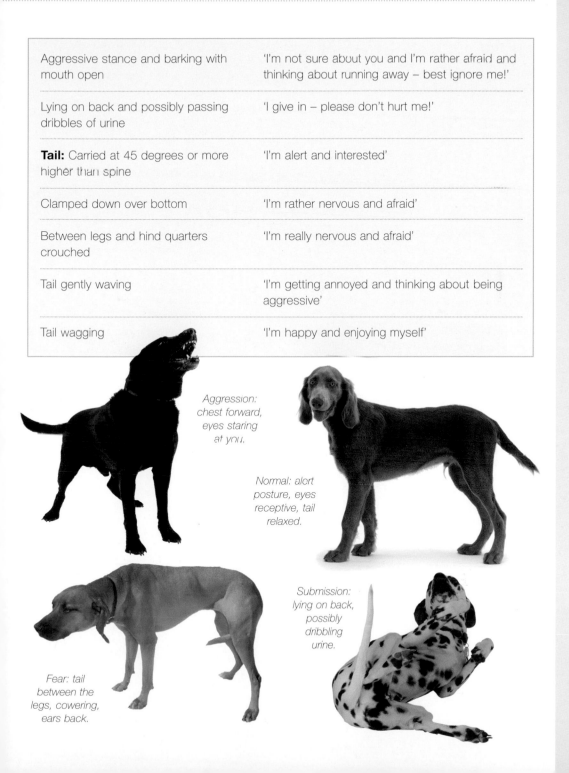

Aggression: chest forward, eyes staring at you.

Normal: alert posture, eyes receptive, tail relaxed.

Fear: tail between the legs, cowering, ears back.

Submission: lying on back, possibly dribbling urine.

HOW DOGS LEARN

Understanding how dogs learn is a fundamental necessity if they are to be taught to respond to specific commands, to be well-mannered and to integrate properly into today's society at large. Essentially dogs learn in two ways: by habituation/socialization and by association.

1. Habituation/ Socialization

Habituation – by this we mean that a dog becomes acclimatized or accustomed to, and accepts, inanimate stimuli such as sounds and objects without fear.

Socialization teaches puppies to accept the presence of people and other animals. Habituation accustoms them to strange sights and sounds.

Socialization – by this we mean that dogs become familiar with, and are happy in the presence of, a variety of people and other animals.

As part of a survival strategy nature ensures that newborn puppies perceive all new experiences as being potentially threatening and instinctively know that evasive action should be taken. Habituation and socialization mean in simple terms 'the loss of such an unlearned, natural, inherent behaviour'. This comes about as the growing pup learns that a particular experience (stimulus), be it the sound of a vacuum cleaner, or the unexpected emergence on its territory of another dog or unfamiliar person, such as the postman, is not, after all, a cause for concern.

If such noises or people are encountered frequently, without untoward result, puppies and older dogs will become 'accustomed' to them and ignore them. The natural response of fearfulness will be lost or at least reduced. This is how effective puppy 'habituation' and 'socialization' works and its importance will be obvious.

It is essential that owners of young puppies make a special effort to familiarize their pet to as many different sounds, animals and people as possible, especially during the first three to four months of its life. It's not too late to habituate and socialize older dogs but in this case especially you must progress slowly and cautiously starting with exposure to soft noises and quiet, unthreatening people and animals. Importantly, each encounter must be positive so that the dog can be rewarded and praised for quiet acceptance. Try to avoid failures, but, if they do occur, go back a stage in the familiarization process.

Quite recently a number of CDs have become available which can be used to familiarize dogs with a great variety of sounds, including thunderstorms and fireworks which can be played at different volume intensities. The instructions given with the CDs must be followed closely if the maximum benefit is to be obtained.

PUPPY HABITUATION AND SOCIALIZATION

Some examples of sounds, objects, people and animals with which dogs should be familiarized.

People	Sounds	Objects	Animals
• Children playing loudly	• Carpet sweepers	• Bicycles	• Cats and
• Crowded streets	• Police, fire and	• Buses	other pets
• Dustmen	ambulance sirens	• Cars	• Cattle
• Men/women	• Fireworks	• Steps and	• Horses
(including vets!)	• Telephones	stairways	• Other dogs
• Postmen	• TV and radio	• Trains	• Sheep
• People with sticks	• Vacuum cleaners		

Close encounters of the bovine kind! A properly socialized dog will not be perturbed by the presence of cattle or other farm animals.

2. Association

Associative learning can involve:
- Conscious thought – in technical terms this is called instrumental conditioning.
- Involuntary reflex actions – this is called classical conditioning.

Instrumental Conditioning

If you reward your dog with a food treat as soon as it has responded correctly to a command, it will learn to repeat the action in anticipation of another reward.

This is the main way dogs learn and simply means that a behaviour is determined by the result it brings. Or, put another way, dogs learn essentially by trial and error. By repetition dogs learn that a certain action will bring a pleasurable experience or an unpleasant result. If the result is pleasurable, the dog learns that the action is worth repeating. If the result is painful or not pleasurable, the dog quickly learns that the action is not worth repeating since it does not 'pay off'!

An important characteristic in respect of trial and error learning is that, because dogs cannot speak, they can't teach one another and they are not able to link a current situation with an event that happened some time previously. As a result, a dog can only establish whether it has done right or wrong if its action brings a reward or 'punishment' within just 0.5–1 second of the event. It is vital to understand and appreciate the significance of this situation if owners are to modify their dog's behaviour and teach it to respond correctly to specific commands.

*Knowing how to use instrumental conditioning can help you to teach a puppy the basic commands, such as **Sit** and **Stay**.*

The information given above should be used to train your dog at least to obey the six major and practical commands: **Sit**, **Down** (lie down), **Stay**, **Heel**, **Come**, and **Leave**, as well as responding, importantly, to **No**, and possibly learning to urinate when it hears an undulating whistle, or some other predetermined sound (see page 21). All these commands should be given briskly and in a tone which demands obedience and prompt action. It is also useful to train your dog to recognize the word **Okay** which you should use to indicate that the desired response can come to an end. In many ways, you should use **Okay** in the same way as 'at ease' is used when soldiers are being drilled.

TRAINING TIPS

- Make training fun
- Set aside two or three sessions daily during the crucial two months after you have homed a puppy or adopted an adult dog, each one lasting five to ten minutes, specifically for formal basic training purposes. Ideally these periods should be between meals and never just before you and your dog are due to go out for a walk or when it is anticipating an exciting event. Your dog will need to be able to concentrate since training is 'work'.
- Some training can take place while your dog is out on a walk as suitable occasions arise but essentially walks are exciting and for the dog's enjoyment not for teaching basic commands. Your dog will be more interested in the surrounding smells and sounds and not in a mood to concentrate.

Rewards, such as praise, a titbit, or a game with a toy, should be given within half a second of the desired action.

- It helps considerably when you start training sessions if you give a command *as the dog is performing the action naturally*. If you see your puppy or older dog about to sit or lie down, give the appropriate command and, once it has completed the action, reward it immediately. (See also Teaching Aids – Tools To Shape Behaviour, page 22.) Dogs soon appreciate that to obey 'pays off'.
- Use gestures *and* words. Motion your puppy into a sitting position, show the flat of your hand for **Stay** and make a downward gesture for **Down** and so on.
- Whatever words and gestures you adopt, don't vary them – *ever*. Make sure that everyone who has contact with the dog conforms precisely, every time.
- Make sure that a good, correct, prompt response to any command is, initially, always rewarded with praise and/or a titbit *without delay*, ideally within just half a second of the action. During the formal training sessions make sure that you have any food rewards you wish to use close to hand. Once the response is learned and well established, give rewards at random intervals to maintain the behaviour but never stop rewards altogether since that can lead to the desired response being extinguished.
- If other members of your family are also going to be involved in training, make sure that everyone uses the same commands and signals. If you don't do this, you risk confusing the dog

Basic Training

It is most important that dogs are trained at the least to respond promptly and obediently to the commands described on these pages if they are to fit without friction into the community at large.

The behaviour modification techniques described earlier in this chapter and the teaching aids described later should be used to establish and maintain the behaviour. Contrary to popular belief, simple behaviour training can start from 10-12 weeks of age; there is no need to wait until the dog reaches adolescence.

Down Give the command using a short sharp tone and insist on instant response. Do *not* use this word to stop dogs jumping up. It is useful to accompany the command with a downward gesture of the arm.

Stay A useful command that can help to ensure that a dog does not run across the road when separated from its owner, for example. Give the command in a sharp tone coupled with a hand held out, palm first. Start training with your dog only a few yards away from you. The distance between you should be increased very gradually so that failures do not occur.

Heel Constant changing of direction during training sessions will help to ensure that the dog does not pull ahead. Sometimes, with big dogs, a face/head collar can be helpful to curb excessive pulling on the lead. It is easier to train dogs to walk to heel as a special exercise rather than while taking a recreational walk.

Come This command is most useful since it can prevent accidents occurring. Training can begin on a long lead to ensure the dog's attention. Never scold a dog that has answered the command to **'Come'** even if it was doing something very wrong when it was called. The word should be voiced in an encouraging way and accompanied by a beckoning gesture.

Sit Ensure that the dog's bottom is properly on the ground and that the response is instantaneous.

It has recently been suggested that giving the commands in a higher pitched voice can help the training process.

Heel Initially heel training is practised with a lead and collar but once a dog becomes adept at walking to heel, the lead can be dispensed with. A well-trained dog will remain focused on its owner and be alert to any changes in speed or direction that may be required.

Tips

- Set aside a few minutes initially each day and subsequently once a week to rehearse and reinforce these commands to ensure that your dog responds promptly and properly.
- Basic training classes can be fun and are of help especially if the dog has been obtained at an older age.

Classical Conditioning

An example of this form of learning is the famous experiment carried out with dogs by the Russian physiologist Ivan Pavlov. He showed that salivation is an automatic reflex response whenever food comes into contact with the mouth. He went on to discover that if a bell is rung consistently at the same time as the food is given, eventually dogs will learn that the sound of the bell heralds the receipt of food and they will begin to salivate in anticipation of feeding. Conditioned dogs will do this at the sound of the bell even when food is not forthcoming.

A more practical illustration of classical conditioning involves house-training of puppies and ensuring that older dogs only urinate outside. If your dog is routinely taken outside when it is likely to want to go to the toilet (either to urinate or defecate), it will associate going out with the reflex body action. If *at the same time* as your dog 'performs' you whistle in an undulating way, it will eventually 'learn' to urinate or defecate when it hears that particular whistle. Such a prompt response can be very useful on cold, dark nights or when stops are made on a car journey!

Sit *A hand signal is useful if you want your dog to sit. Make sure its bottom is on the ground.*

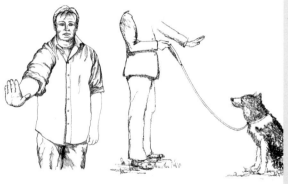

Stay *It is important that a dog is taught to stay securely and consistently without moving.*

Come *A dog must learn to come when called – its safety could one day depend upon it.*

Down *The down position is comfortable for a dog and so useful if it has to remain still for some time.*

STAGES IN A PUPPY'S DEVELOPMENT

In respect of future behaviour and understanding how to teach dogs, it is important to recognize that puppies go through a number of key stages during their development.

Neonatal period	2–4 weeks ± 1 week
Primary habituation/socialization period	4–7 weeks ± 1 week
General habituation/socialization period	8–12 weeks ± 1 week
Critical period for sensitivity	8–12 weeks ± 1 week

During the neonatal period puppies are looked after principally by their mother but some supervision by the breeder is needed to ensure that all is well and that the puppy is sucking, urinating and defecating normally.

Owners of young puppies should maximize the use of the habituation/socialization periods since at this time the puppies are at the height of their learning ability. A dog's future development and stability depends very much on careful and sympathetic handling during these periods. Much thought is needed to ensure that each new experience is a happy one. Inappropriate (or lack of) habituation and socialization may be the cause of:

- Fear-related aggression to people or other animals
- Phobias or avoidance behaviour
- Separation anxiety – fear of being left alone
- An abnormal interaction with the dog's owner – sometimes over-attachment!

These Boxer puppies are eight weeks old (top) and 12 weeks old (below). This is the optimum period for habituation and socialization training.

Towards the end of the primary habituation/socialization period the breeder or owner should start the house-training process.

Great care must be taken to avoid, or at least minimize, fearful experiences during the critical period for sensitivity. Punishment must never be used at this time in a dog's life.

TEACHING AIDS – TOOLS TO SHAPE BEHAVIOUR

In simple terms owners have available four main aids or methods (tools) which can be used to teach dogs. If these are applied correctly and promptly, dogs will respond in the desired way surprisingly quickly. If used consistently by *everyone* in contact with the pet, dogs can be taught to do virtually anything within their physical ability.

1. Rewards

Food A coveted titbit, dog chocolate drops, or small pieces of meat or cheese can be used very effectively as a reward for the

Food titbits, promptly given, help to reinforce desired behaviour.

desired response to a command. However, since the reward needs to be given very promptly, wrapped food is of little use. The dog will not make the association between the command and its response if it has to wait for the reward to be unwrapped!

Praise Dogs regard as praise any form of attention including petting, stroking etc., especially if accompanied by enthusiastic verbal encouragement. It is important to take care that actions which the dog may perceive as praise are not made inadvertently when the dog is misbehaving. If this is done, the inappropriate behaviour will soon become part of the dog's repertoire.

2. Chastisement – Punishment

Praise, such as petting and stroking accompanied by enthusiastic words of encouragement, is a potent reward for a dog.

Essentially punishment can take three forms. It can involve the administration of a painful stimulus in a direct or an indirect way, or the withdrawal of something that the dog finds pleasurable.

The Administration of a Painful Stimulus In this context the severity of punishment will need to be varied according to the pet's size and temperament. Punishment must never be cruel nor should it ever be used in temper. Ideally too it can be helpful to give your dog the chance to adopt an alternative acceptable learned behaviour which will bring a reward. If punishment is used, you must follow the rules summarized in the box on page 24.

Magic Punishment So-called 'magic punishment' can be very effective indeed. A suitable object, such as a bean-bag, thrown from a hiding place which strikes a dog *while a 'crime' is actually being committed* is very useful. This is because the dog will not link the punishment with you (the dog perceives that it is being punished by the environment) and it is immediate and unpredictable. Its effectiveness also highlights the value of 'set-up' situations, where an owner anticipates the wrongdoing and is ready to administer punishment *as the act is committed* – there is no delay and the dog cannot help but make the association between cause and effect. Water pistols can be used in a similar way. Alternatively training discs or a tin containing marbles or pebbles thrown onto the ground behind a dog to make a startling sound can also be used to interrupt an unwanted behaviour.

The Withdrawal of Something Pleasurable Simply ignoring your dog, giving it no attention at all and showing your displeasure by your body language will often be sufficient to teach it that there is no point in repeating the undesirable behaviour. If this is not enough, banishing your dog to a room on its own and ignoring it for a short while can also be effective. In this context it is important not to make your dog's bed a place of punishment; it is its place of rest, not a cell!

RULES GOVERNING THE USE OF PUNISHMENT

- Apply the punishment consistently, fairly and without delay. This usually takes the form of a mild slap with your hand on the dog's body (but certainly not on the dog's head or involving the use of a stick).
- Use punishment which is strong enough to disrupt the undesirable behaviour but which does not cause suffering or is prolonged.
- Do not punish shy, nervous dogs or puppies less than 12 weeks of age; in such cases a firm **'No'** accompanied by disapproving body language will usually be enough.

- A quick firm tap on the nose may be effective in the case of larger dogs but care should be taken that such an action is not confused with play since that can be completely counter-productive and may even encourage aggression or anxiety.
- It can be helpful to give your dog the chance to adopt on command another learned behaviour which will bring a reward when completed properly.
- If you have any doubts about the appropriateness of punishment, it is better to ignore the behaviour.

3. Relying On Extinction

If you have any doubt about which of the training methods should be used, it is best to ignore the behaviour. It is far better to do nothing than to get it wrong. Relying on an inappropriate behaviour being extinguished (forgotten) is often a safe option with many dogs and especially those with a tendency to dominance.

Finally it is worth noting that the rather more traditional training method described thus far is simple, straightforward and works; it has been tried and tested and is applicable in a family situation allowing everyone in contact with the dog to be involved.

4. Other Training Aids

Clicker Training With this method the dog first learns to associate a two-toned click with getting a reward (a titbit and/or praise). Once this connection is established, the clicker can be used to make the dog aware that its behaviour is what its owner wants. If the method is to be effective, it is important to click while the behaviour is actually being performed – *not* after it has been completed. Timing the click with precision is essential for success. There is no doubt that this training method works but its value *in a family situation* must be open to question. This is because clicker training requires an in-depth understanding of what is involved, split-second timing, and considerable dedication. The method is not really something that can be easily undertaken and shared by all members of a family. Furthermore, it is hardly applicable in dog training classes.

The clatter of the training discs hitting the ground can distract a dog that is not behaving as you would like.

Deterrent sprays can be applied to objects that a dog habitually chews – such as its lead or a shoe – to try to discourage this behaviour. However, their value is debatable – there is no guarantee that the dog will not continue to chew items that have not been sprayed.

Training Discs Training discs can, theoretically, be used in two main ways. First, they can be thrown to the ground to distract a dog that is misbehaving and thus disrupt its behaviour. This can be helpful – at least in some cases, for example preventing jumping up or possibly chasing cats. Secondly, it is suggested that the dog learns that the noise made by discs as they hit the ground is associated with an unwanted behaviour. The dog starts to associate the sound with the command **'No'**.

Clickers and training discs suffer from the disadvantage that they will not always be immediately available at the time of need. So it is probably better and simpler to use from the start a distinctive loud hand clap together with a clearly spoken, sharp **'No'** followed by giving the command for an acceptable behaviour which allows the dog to 'escape' into a situation that will 'pay off'.

Deterrent Sprays A number of sprays containing an unpleasant smelling liquid are recommended by some behaviourists, especially to discourage young puppies from chewing objects such as shoes or children's toys. They have also been advocated to help prevent dominant dogs from jumping up at people (especially young children). This system, however, does have its limitations because it could teach the dog that it should only *not* chew sprayed items and *not* jump up at sprayed individuals!

Dog-appeasing Pheromone (DAP) (Pheromone therapy)
Pheromones are chemicals that are given off by animals into the environment. They are picked up usually by other members of the same species by inhalation or by direct contact and bring about a change in attitude, or the development of a particular behaviour. They have been referred to as 'social odours'.

Dog-appeasing pheromone is a synthetic pheromone which is delivered into the environment through an electronic 'plug-in' diffuser or as a spray. DAP replicates the signals of 'well-being' generated by the natural pheromone produced by the skin surrounding the mammary glands in lactating bitches. It is claimed that problems such as destructive behaviour, excessive barking, house soiling and excessive licking are reduced in severity when DAP is used. DAP is only available through veterinary surgeons whose advice as to whether or not it is likely to be of benefit in your situation and exactly how it should be used is critical.

REINFORCEMENT –

Establishing & Maintaining a Learned Behaviour

- Learning is achieved more quickly if the response is rewarded (reinforced) every time a command is obeyed promptly and correctly.
- Intermittent, random, strong reinforcement (big rewards) are most effective in *maintaining* a desired behaviour once it is learned.
- Any behaviours you have taught your dog are much more likely to be maintained if you continue to ensure that your dog sees you as the 'elected leader' and respects your wishes.

DOMINANCE AND SUBMISSIVENESS –

Your Leadership Role

Some puppies are extroverts, tending to be dominant and pushy, others tend to be introverted and shy. Occasionally the former can become threatening and in guard dogs that can be a problem. If this is happening with your puppy, start to carry out the exercises described below once or twice a week until you have no cause for concern, and then occasionally, say once or twice a month.

Alternatively your pet may be too submissive, as evidenced by it lying on its back and exposing its abdomen or urinating involuntarily when it thinks you are cross, or even just unhappy with its behaviour. In this case you should consistently ignore the dog when such signs are seen. You can help to boost your dog's confidence by allowing it to put its forelegs on your shoulders briefly when you are in a kneeling or crouching position, and by giving it a few extra privileges.

The exercises described below may also be applied with caution to older dogs but if they result in a real confrontation, it is best to seek expert advice.

Exercises For Asserting Your Leadership Role

- Stand over your dog from behind, lift its front legs off the ground and keep them off the ground for 30-45 seconds. Reward the dog with spoken praise if it remains still and quiet, but rebuke any struggling.
- Place the dog on its side and hold it there with one hand on its muzzle, keeping its mouth shut, and the other pressing down firmly on its chest. Hold it in that position for 30-45 seconds and give praise or rebuke the dog verbally as appropriate.
- Reinstate or step up the basic training exercises (see page 20). Be very particular that your dog responds quickly and properly

to the basic commands. Do not tolerate any hesitation. Reward good behaviour lavishly.

- Finally, ignore your dog if it begs in any way, or seeks praise when it has not been earned. Turn your back meaningfully, don't say a word. Do this every time. If you are not consistent your dog will certainly try it on again in the hope that you may respond again favourably by giving it some attention, which it will perceive as praise!

These exercises can help to establish and maintain your leadership role in the case of pets that have a tendency to dominance. If the dog shows signs of aggression, however, seek expert help.

CONCLUSION

The information provided, correctly and consistently applied in relation to your dog's demeanour, will enable you to eliminate inappropriate behaviour, prevent the establishment of undesirable behaviour in your dog, 'train' it to respond properly and promptly to basic commands, and shape its behaviour to meet your particular requirements. As a result you will be able to mould it quickly and effectively into a happy, contented dog that fits snugly into your family group and into the community at large.

A well-trained dog is a delight to be with and a source of fun and pleasure for all the family.

Finally do understand that there really is no need to put up with unacceptable behaviour. Resolve to do something about it if you are unhappy; don't be tempted to turn a blind eye or make excuses. If you can't establish the cause of the problem or if your dog fails to respond to the course of action you decide on, seek professional help from a trained dog behaviourist or veterinary surgeon. Finally, a word of warning – ***don't try to solve a problem of aggression to people on your own*** – seek qualified professional help from the outset.

SOLVING COMMON BEHAVIOURAL PROBLEMS

If you have adopted an adult dog, it possibly has an established behaviour that you do not find acceptable. And even if you have followed the advice given earlier about behaviour training, it is still possible that your dog will adopt some undesirable behaviour. In either case, use your newly acquired knowledge of how dogs think and learn, and the methods by which dog behaviour can be shaped, to overcome the problem. You should often be able to 'do it yourself'. Start by considering the questions noted below. If these are answered truthfully, you should be able to identify the cause and the solution will become clear.

Step 1 Try to analyse the situation carefully. What exactly does the dog do? Does the behaviour occur regularly, apparently at random, or is it associated with some specific event? For how long has it been going on? Have you recently changed any routine? Is the dog left on its own more frequently or for longer periods of time than previously? Are you at home less often, maybe as a result of becoming newly employed or through a change of job? Has there been any other change to family life, such as the arrival of a new baby or another pet?

You don't have to put up with problem behaviours, like excessive barking. Even if they seem to be deeply rooted, there are ways of improving the situation.

Step 2 Examine your attitude to your dog and that of everyone who has regular contact with it. Are you or someone else inadvertently rewarding your dog when it behaves in a way that you don't approve of? Remember that most dogs regard any attention as praise even though it may be intended as chastisement or firm punishment!

Step 3 Consider whether, as a result of leniency or insufficient attention, your dog has become too dominant and too pushy. Is someone applying inappropriate punishment or being too liberal with titbits and favours? Could the problem be sexually motivated in the case of male dogs? Have some corrective procedures already been applied and failed? Were they really appropriate?

Step 4 Once the cause has been identified, make the necessary change(s) and outline a plan of action for everyone who is involved with the dog to overcome the problem and prevent the situation occurring again.

Step 5 If you are unable to establish a likely cause of the problem, or the actions you take and the changes you make do not prove to be effective, seek help sooner rather than later. Your vet or an experienced animal behaviourist may well be able to help. *Always* seek help if the problem involves aggression towards people.

What if my dog barks excessively?

1 Such behaviour is really irritating and can quickly lead to conflict between neighbours. Short-lived barking as a warning is fine but ongoing long-lasting barking is annoying and disruptive.

Remedial Action: Never encourage barking by saying things such as 'What's that?' in an excited voice when a noise is heard. Ignore the dog when it barks and make no physical contact with it at all; to do so could be regarded by the dog as praise. Make sure that the dog is not being left on its own frequently or for too long. If the dog is left alone, turn the radio on. If the dog barks in your presence, give the command **'Down'** and say 'Be quiet'. Reward it for obeying promptly. The objective is to teach the dog that lying down quietly 'pays off', whereas barking does not – barking from a lying position is difficult. See also Separation anxiety, 'What if?' no.15, page 36.

What if my dog bites and nips at people's hands and ankles?

2 This behaviour is sometimes a development of an innate behaviour in herding dogs like Corgis. It needs to be stopped before people are hurt.

Remedial Action: Command **'No'** sharply and/or give mild punishment *as the crime is committed*, followed by social isolation and the withdrawal of favours – the behaviour should extinguish. Reinstate basic training exercises and start carrying out the leadership/dominance exercises described earlier in this section to ensure that your dog knows that *you* are in charge.

What if my dog chews favourite family items?

3 Puppies often explore their surroundings by chewing objects within their vicinity. If this behaviour continues, significant damage can be done to items that you value, thus prompt remedial action is called for.

Remedial Action: Give your puppy only one or two specific objects to chew (e.g. a special toy or raw-hide chew). If your dog goes to chew something else, distract it with a command such as **'Sit'**, and praise it for responding properly. Substitute the chewed item with an acceptable object. Make a firm effort to remove all temptation in the future. Don't give your dog old shoes as toys, for example, for it will not be able to differentiate old from new. This problem is one that lends itself to be cured by a 'set-up' situation using 'magic punishment' (see page 23).

What if my dog is agressive towards people, strangers and possibly family members?

4

Prompt action is needed to stamp out any tendency towards aggression before someone is seriously hurt. **Remedial Action:** Seek professional help. Sometimes such aggression can be stopped but it is vital to establish and eliminate the cause, possibly pain, fear or simply excessive dominance or over-guarding behaviour. If this is not done properly, the dog may never be trustworthy in this respect. If you have young children in your house or nearby, take extra care and be prepared for the fact that your dog may need to be destroyed. Re-homing it is not really a fair option.

What if my dog shows hypersexual traits?

5

The behaviours noted in the table below are considered to be associated with hypersexuality.

Behaviour	Likely effectiveness of castration
Aggression	60% (inter-male); 0% (other cases)
Mounting inanimate objects and people	70%
Territory marking about the home	50%
Roaming	90-100%
Destructiveness	Very variable
Excitability	Very variable

Hypersexual behaviour may involve the mounting of inanimate objects.

Remedial Action: Make sure that you are not inadvertently reinforcing the behaviour. Be sure that your dog gets plenty of quality exercise. Remove temptations and opportunity, and ensure that your property is properly fenced. Give your dog plenty of physical and mental exercise. Consult your vet.

In dogs that have not yet reached adolescence, behaviour training methods aimed at increasing your leadership role can be useful. If your dog even looks like behaving in this way, a firm **'No'** or a thrown object coupled with the command **'Sit'** (which when obeyed can be rewarded) will soon teach the dog that such actions certainly don't 'pay off'. In adult dogs, chemical or surgical castration can be of help, perhaps combined with other medical treatment. See also Castration of dogs in Part 3, 'What if? no.102 and Territory marking in Part 2, 'What if?' no.28.

What if my dog is jealous of another dog that I own?

6 This is quite a common problem, especially when two dogs of the same sex are kept together and is one reason why many veterinary surgeons don't recommend that owners keep more than one pet dog. Not only can the dogs cause damage to each other, but if they are separated while fighting, people can only too easily be injured.

Remedial Action: Enhance your leadership position over both dogs (see page 27). The situation can be helped by increasing the status of the more dominant dog with the objective of encouraging the underdog to accept its subservient role, and so become more contented and comfortable. The dominant dog should be fed first, given more attention, and receive more favours. If you see a fight about to develop, give the command **'Down'** to both dogs and reward prompt obedience. Consider also using 'magic punishment' with a thrown object or use training discs or a water pistol to distract the dogs.

What if my dog jumps up at people?

7 This behaviour is a real 'turn off' for many people, especially if your dog is wet or has muddy paws. With perseverance, however, it can be overcome by taking the actions noted below.

Remedial Action: Try to stop this behaviour through extinction. When the dog jumps up, quickly turn away with arms folded and ignore it. If you can see the warning signs, quickly tell your dog to **'Sit'** and then reward it. Apply this consistently and your dog should soon learn that it only receives attention when it is sitting quietly. Tell visitors to avoid as far as possible giving your dog the chance to jump up. Above all, they must not touch it in any way. If your dog looks like it is about to jump up at a visitor, try 'magic punishment' or distract its attention by dropping training discs or a tin containing marbles behind it. Give a command such as **'Sit'** and reward a correct response. Note the command **'Down'** means 'lie down' not 'don't jump up'! In some cases it helps if visitors who arrive by car greet the dog from their car seats before getting out of the vehicle and giving it the chance to jump up at them.

What if my dog chases people (especially those on bicycles) and animals?

8

The dangers to people and other dogs of this problem are obvious. Take time and effort to stop it occurring once and for all.

Remedial Action: Spend as much time as you can on obedience training. It ought to be sufficient if you practise for two 5-minute sessions twice daily for two weeks, then once daily for a further two weeks, then hopefully just once a week or at a longer interval. Make sure that your dog responds properly and promptly. Concentrate on the commands **'Come'** and **'No'**. Carry out the leadership/dominance exercises illustrated on page 27. Use a thrown object, a jet of water or training discs to distract the dog and stop it as it is about to take off. Use a 'set-up' situation so that you can use 'magic punishment'. This can be very effective with dogs that chase people on bicycles. It can also be helpful to get a colleague to ride past your dog. If it starts to chase, the rider should stop immediately and admonish the dog, possibly using a water pistol or something similar. In those circumstances the dog will have lost and the 'game' will no longer be fun.

A quick squirt with a water pistol would soon cool his enthusiasm! Sudden shocks like that can prove effective in interrupting chase behaviour.

What if my dog is overly submissive?

9

Submissive behaviour, which can sometimes lead to a dog lying on its back to expose its abdomen while dribbling urine involuntarily, can be very embarrassing for an owner. It is certainly undesirable and a situation that you should try to remedy.

Remedial Action: Build up your dog's confidence by giving it some extra privileges and letting it begin to lead (see page 26).

Aggression towards other dogs is a serious problem. You must not allow such behaviour to continue unchecked.

What if my dog is aggressive to other dogs?

10 Your dog will soon get a bad reputation if it even threatens other dogs when they meet. This behaviour is a big cause for concern and an embarrassment and worry for owners. Don't make excuses for your dog; accept that it has a problem and resolve to do something about it.

Remedial Action: Avoid contact with other dogs wherever possible except those that are known to be friendly, and build up gradually so that your dog begins to accept contact with more and more different types of dog. Progress slowly and try to avoid failure. If you don't succeed, go back a stage in the process and start again. If a dog is seen approaching when on a walk, cross to the other side of the road and start giving the command **'Leave'** as early as possible, followed by **'Sit'** and **'Stay'**, accompanied by an appropriate hand gesture. Make your dog look at you to distract it and reward it for being quiet as the other dog passes. In male dogs chemical or surgical castration may help in some persistent cases – your vet will advise. See 'What if?' no.5 and also Part 2, 'What if?' no.55.

What if my dog is disobedient and won't come when called?

11 This is an embarrassment that needs remedying promptly and permanently.

Remedial Action: Increase your leadership status (see page 27) and reinstate formal basic command training exercises as described on page 20. Pay particular attention to the command **'Come'**, making use of an extending lead. Make a correct prompt response seem very attractive with lots of praise and delectable titbits. Clapping your hands firmly (but not aggressively in the way that is done to reinforce the command **'No'**) to attract your dog's attention before calling it can be useful since your dog will see the movement of your hands from a distance as well as hearing the sound. Very often it will soon learn that a clap means 'if I return promptly, I will get a reward'.

What if my dog suffers from car sickness?

12 Dogs that travel badly are a worry to owners not only because of the inconvenience of having to clean up but also because they can so readily cause friction between the occupants of the car and possibly be the cause of a road traffic accident.

Remedial Action: Dogs can suffer from true motion sickness, and if that is the case, you will need to obtain suitable medication from your veterinary surgeon. Some cars may be more inclined to make dogs sick than others, and this can be worth checking before any other action is taken. More often, however, car sickness stems from anxiety on the part of the dog, possibly as a result of a previous bad experience. In such cases, accustom the dog to the car while it is stationary in the driveway, and let the dog get in and out freely; provide a comfortable cushion for it on the back seat. Once the dog is happy, let it get in the car when it is tired and just drive round the block. As long as the dog is happy and relaxed, gradually increase the distance covered. If the dog drools or whines, ignore it completely – next time reduce the distance and start again.

Car sickness is often an anxious reaction to being in a vehicle. You must try to get your dog to accept the car as a safe haven where it feels relaxed and secure.

Make sure that the first longer trips in the car are enjoyable, ending up with a walk at a favourite place. Ideally you should aim to make your car your dog's 'second home'. A place where you can put it safely and happily if, for example, you have workmen in the house or visitors who don't like dogs. Finally two words of warning – don't leave your dog alone in the car with children. Although it may be trustworthy as far as aggression is concerned, it could cause injury by pacing backwards and forwards if it feels that someone is about to invade its territory and harm 'its' children. Never, ever drive with your dog's head out of the car window; it is dangerous and could harm your dog's eyes.

What if my dog eats its own faeces or those of other animals?

13 Coprophagia is an extremely off-putting and embarrassing habit which seems almost to be an inbuilt trait in some dogs. It can often lead to owners becoming cross with their pet and shouting at it. Since the habit may possibly cause digestive upsets, it is important to resolve to stop the behaviour.

Remedial Action: Remove the temptation by picking up

promptly any faeces in the garden. Watch your dog closely when walking in fields. Use the **'Leave'** command if it even looks at animal droppings. Call **'Come'**, command **'Sit'** and reward your dog when it responds correctly. Take with you a suitable object, such as a bean bag, to throw at your dog if it is some distance away and shout **'No'** *as it is about to eat the offending material*. Your dog should soon learn that such an action most certainly does not 'pay off'. Subsequently, as soon as you enter a field, you should say to your dog 'don't even think about eating that'. With the right body language that warning should be enough.

Coprophagia is a distinctly unsavoury habit; it may also cause gastric problems.

What if my dog is too dominant?

14 If excessive dominant behaviour is allowed to persist, it can often develop into aggression to people or destructiveness. Thus immediate action is needed to curb the trait and to prevent it occurring again over the long term.

Remedial Action: Carry out the leadership exercises described on pages 26-7 and step up the basic training exercises noted on page 20. Make certain that privileges are only ever given when they have been earned. Be very careful about using direct punishment; it is better to ignore the behaviour than risk getting your response wrong. If you play games with your dog, make certain that *you* always win. Don't play tug of war games; they may well encourage active dominance over you or outright aggressive behaviour.

What if my dog suffers from separation anxiety and is over-anxious and destructive when left alone in the house or car?

15 It is very important that you can leave your dog on its own in the house or your car without worry. You need to know that it will stay quietly without causing any damage or trying to escape. Destructive behaviour caused by separation anxiety is sadly one of the most common reasons for dogs being sent to a rescue centre or 'put down'.

Prevention:

- If you home a puppy, start getting it used to being left alone when it is 12-14 weeks old. If you adopt an adult older dog, start within the first week or two of taking it home.
- Make sure that your dog is comfortable in its bed in the house or on a cushion or bean bag on the back seat of your car. The bed can be placed in a dog crate if you are using one.
- Ensure that your dog is tired and not hungry, so that it is more inclined to sleep, and that it has been taken out to relieve itself shortly before you depart.
- Decide on specific actions you are always going to take when you leave your dog alone in the house; this might be turning on the radio softly, turning on a low light or giving your dog a favourite toy which is kept for this purpose only. These actions will serve as a valuable cue to the dog that you will inevitably return after a variable period of time.
- Make sure that your dog has water, that the place is adequately ventilated and is not likely to get too hot or cold.
- As you leave, talk to your dog in a normal voice saying things like 'There's a good dog', 'I won't be long' and give it a quick pat. Although the dog will not understand the words, it will soon recognize the tone and the way you say it and that will reinforce the dog's understanding that you will return. Try not to vary in any way what you do and say; consistency is very important. You may, if you like, give your dog a small treat, maybe half a sweet biscuit, as you leave.
- Start by leaving your dog for very short periods, maybe only five minutes, making sure your dog has noted the adopted cue(s). Don't go far, keep out of sight and preferably remain within earshot. If all is well on your return and you have not heard your dog bark or whine in your absence, reward your dog with a favourite titbit and give lavish verbal praise.

Before you leave the house, settle your dog down on its familiar bed. If it feels safe and comfortable, it will be happier while left on its own.

Bouts of destructive behaviour caused by separation anxiety put an intense strain on the dog/owner relationship.

- Over the next seven to 14 days gradually increase the interval for which you are absent by five to ten minutes at a time, up to a total duration of two hours. Initially it is sensible to wait somewhere out of your dog's sight but from where you can hear it so that you can return promptly should your dog start to bark, whine or become excitable. Should that happen, go back, ignore the behaviour, settle your dog down and go through the chosen procedure, but leave the dog for a shorter period of time and start to lengthen the separation period more gradually.
- Finally, if you make up to eight such 'practice' departures daily over three to four days you will, provided you have no failures on the way, be able in less than a week to leave your dog safely for at least an hour. However, don't set your expectations too high, as that may result in you rushing the procedure. And remember that some dogs are not such quick learners as others.

What if my dog pulls on the lead?

16 There is little more exhausting than a dog that pulls on the lead but you do not need to suffer in this way. Certainly you must not keep jerking on the lead and then giving a command afterwards, as so many people do. Your dog will have no idea what it is all about.

Remedial Action: Train your dog to walk closely by your left side while holding the lead loosely in your right hand. Keep changing direction as you walk along during a training session; that will help to prevent your dog from pulling since it will be unsure about what you are going to do next. Remember to give the dog a chance to respond to the command **'Heel'** first and then give a gentle tug on the lead if necessary – not the other way round. It can help to establish the behaviour and to reinforce the command silently if you tap your thigh lightly with your left hand as you say **'Heel'**. This sound and gesture may well eventually replace the need to say the word **'Heel'** on every occasion.

If you are not making progress, consider obtaining a head/face collar. That may help by giving you more control over a persistent puller; if not, try joining a dog training class or seek help from a trained dog behaviourist.

What if my dog is shy with other people?

17

Shy dogs are embarrassing and make it difficult for people to know how to react. Your dog will miss out on the friendly greeting that well-behaved dogs elicit.

Remedial Action: Teach the dog that it is more rewarding to **'Sit'** in situations where it might be shy, and reward a correct response lavishly. Do not use punishment if your dog is shy. It is better to ignore the behaviour and work on building up its confidence by giving a few privileges. Don't let people force themselves on your dog; let the dog set the pace. Initially ask people to approach your dog quietly and avoid making sudden expansive gestures.

What if my dog licks people's hands excessively?

18

Some people like this attention but most don't, so it is better to teach your dog that such behaviour is not acceptable and does not 'pay off'.

Remedial Action: Family members and visitors should positively ignore the dog if it attempts this behaviour and give it no opportunity to act in this way. Frequently this is a sign of over-submissiveness and it can help to follow the advice given on page 32.

What if my dog begs for food or attention?

19

Importantly you must train your dog that begging is not allowed. If the behaviour is allowed even occasionally, then it will soon become established. Your dog will take advantage of well-intentioned visitors and you will be on a slippery slope.

Remedial Action: Rely on extinction; make it a house rule that everyone who has any contact with the dog must ignore the behaviour and certainly never ever give the dog an unearned titbit. A well-trained dog should not even *think* about begging.

Dogs are smart when it comes to playing on our emotions, but do harden your heart to those doleful eyes and entreating looks. If you start giving a dog unearned treats and titbits, you are on a slippery slope.

What if my dog is possessive over food?

20 It is a natural trait for dogs to guard food as they would do in the wild. However, this behaviour is not acceptable in a domestic household, especially if there are children present. This action could easily lead to your dog causing serious injury to family members and becoming over-dominant in other ways. It is vital that your dog learns that you not only give food, toys and other objects but that you are also 'entitled' to take them away.

Remedial Action:

- Do not retaliate or threaten your dog with punishment. You could lose, and that would make the situation worse.
- Start by giving meals that are less palatable to your dog; this will make it less inclined to guard its bowl.
- Remove the feeding bowl promptly when your dog has finished eating. Do this when it is looking, not behind its back.
- Step up the training and leadership exercises noted earlier paying particular attention to the **'No'** command.

What if my dog is inclined to steal food?

21 Essentially dogs do not understand the concept of stealing; if food is left available, it is there for the taking. This is a natural inbuilt action not necessarily driven by hunger, although some dogs are prone to gluttony (Labradors are often a special problem in this respect).

Remedial Action:

- Inform everyone in the household that they must not leave food lying around – remove all likely temptation.
- Consider using a 'set-up' scenario coupled with 'magic punishment'.
- Increase your leadership status (see pages 26-7).
- Give your dog plenty of physical and mental exercise.
- Ensure that you are feeding your dog the right quantity of a well-balanced diet.

What if my dog is not fully house-trained?

22 House rule number one has to be that dogs do not urinate in the house, for any reason! There is absolutely no need to put up with this habit and make excuses for the animal, except, of course, if it is unwell.

Remedial Action: House-Training – Puppies

Essentially two methods of house-training your puppy are recommended. There are those who advise that the pup should be trained to go initially on newspaper placed near the back door and then subsequently educated to go outside, possibly first on newspaper and then in the same place after the paper has been removed. Others consider that it is better to go for broke in the first instance. This method has the advantage that training is needed only once, the goal is realistic and if the principles noted below are followed meticulously, the desired result can be achieved in a remarkably short period of time. Placing your puppy's bed in an indoor crate or playpen can be helpful since dogs generally do not like to urinate or defecate near their sleeping place or near where they eat.

First it is essential that you are willing, able and dedicated enough to monitor and supervise your puppy closely *all the time* for the first five to seven days or so in your house. You can of course take time out when the puppy is deeply asleep and delegation of responsibility to other members of the family is allowed as long as they are also diligent and follow the set rules.

One school of thought recommends first training a puppy to go to the toilet on newspaper indoors, and then moving the paper outside.

The essential steps to success are these:

1 Give your puppy as much opportunity as possible to go to the toilet outside and reduced opportunity to soil in the house by taking it outside at least every 90 minutes or so during the day.

2 Make up your mind that the puppy is not going to 'blot its copy book' – ever.

3 Familiarize yourself with the signs that your puppy will show when it is *thinking about* going to the toilet. Usually the puppy will start by being restless, circling round and round and finally beginning to crouch. If you see such signs or even suspect the puppy is thinking of 'going', act promptly and take the puppy outside without delay.

4 When outside, as your puppy 'performs' make the undulating whistle mentioned on page 21, or employ another command or phrase if you prefer, to encourage it to urinate or defecate. Immediately the pup has finished continue the whistle for a little longer and give lavish praise – verbally and by petting. Providing it's immediately available, you can give a food reward too. The puppy will soon learn to connect the whistle or other command with going to the toilet.

5 Remember that puppies will inevitably want to go to the toilet when they wake up. If your puppy has had a snooze, take it outside straight away and follow the routine described above.

6 Similarly, puppies will want to relieve themselves soon after a meal and possibly after a period of play. Be prepared to act as noted above soon after the puppy has finished eating or when a period of play or excitement is over.

7 Current opinion is that it is not best practice to stick to one particular place or specific surface when encouraging your pup to go to the toilet outside. To do so could be counter-productive in the future when the surface it is used to performing on is not available. If you have trained your puppy to eliminate on just grass or gravel, you could have a big problem if you stop at a motorway service station or garage forecourt. Better to encourage your dog from the start to 'go' on any surface except, maybe, the flowerbeds!

8 Importantly every member of your family must be prepared to take turns on 'puppy watch' and follow the procedure you have adopted, *to the letter*.

9 Finally if you happen to have a failure, don't scold the puppy, simply mop up and resolve not to let it happen again. Because puppies will be naturally drawn back to areas where they have urinated or defecated previously, it makes sense to remove any scent from the area by using one of the effective odour-eliminating and stain-removing products that are available. You will be surprised what progress you can make, even in a matter of just a few days. ▶

If you are attentive, you should be able to spot when your puppy starts to circle and crouch down in preparation for urination. In such circumstances, take the puppy outside immediately.

Remedial Action: House-Training – Adult Dogs

With adult dogs that blot their copybook the first step must be to ensure that the problem is not associated with some disease or condition, such as cystitis, kidney problems, diabetes, imminent heat in bitches or hypersexuality in dogs etc. If you suspect that this could be the case, seek veterinary help to establish the cause. Consider too whether the problem is the result of the lack of house-training previously, or through misdirected training methods. In this case the steps noted above for training puppies should be followed although obviously adult dogs need not be taken out so frequently to start with (see step 1).

As with other behavioural problems it is sensible to carry out the leadership exercises regularly and set aside time for regular basic training. This will ensure that your dog regards you as being the outright leader and someone it would rather die for than annoy in any way.

What if my dog resents being groomed?

23 This behaviour is most commonly due to your dog trying to become more dominant and exert its authority over you. However, it can sometimes be the result of the process causing pain, e.g. if the dog has a wound, an ear problem or arthritis. If you think this could be the case, especially if the problem has just arisen in a normally well-behaved dog, try to locate the painful area, if necessary seeking veterinary help.

I WISH SHE'D STOP DOING THAT!

Remedial Action:

- Correct any underlying medical cause.
- Reinforce your leadership status (see pages 26-7).
- Be less vigorous about grooming, having first ascertained that your grooming tools are not too sharp or abrasive. Concentrate on those areas that are more acceptable to your dog, like its back for example, and progress slowly to more sensitive areas. Always reward good acceptance behaviour. Try to ensure that you don't have failures on the way; if you do, go back a step or two and start again.

When a previously compliant dog starts to react badly while being groomed, it is possible that something is causing it pain.

What if my dog has a phobia?

24

A phobia is an excessive fear of certain stimuli, such as noises, flashes of light, certain types of people, other animals or possibly just being left alone. Such an inappropriate and excessive response to a stimulus can lead to serious injury to the animal and sometimes its owner or other people. Furthermore, considerable damage to property can result from the frantic attempts by a dog affected in this way to 'escape'.

Dogs that have undergone careful and comprehensive habituation and socialization should not exhibit an excessive fear response to everyday stimuli. However, it is not always possible to cover all eventualities and it is not uncommon for some dogs, especially those of an introvert nature, to develop exaggerated signs of stress or anxiety in unusual situations, such as during thunderstorms, or when fireworks are being let off. Indeed, it is now considered that excessive fearfulness is a trait that can be inherited. However, it is also true that such behaviour can be the result of inappropriate actions by the owner. This is often the case with fireworks since the natural instinct of the owner is to pet and cuddle their dog when it is fearful. This will inevitably be 'read' by the dog as a reward or praise and it will, as a result, continue to shake and shiver to an even greater extent at the time and on future occasions.

Many phobias are probably best prevented by thinking ahead, by careful habituation and socialization and by a thoughtful response by the owner when signs of fear are shown. If that fails, as can so easily happen, especially with introverted pets, it will be necessary to think in terms of short-term management and, importantly, to use behaviour modification techniques to prevent the problem in the future.

Short-Term Management

If your dog shows phobic signs for the first time during a thunderstorm or when fireworks are being let off, try the following procedure if the dog's reaction is not too severe. As soon as your dog starts to shiver, shake and pace about the house, shut the doors and windows and draw the curtains, take your dog into the lounge and turn on the TV or radio as loudly as you can stand to mask the noise outside as much as possible. Do not fuss over, try to calm, touch or pay any attention to your dog, since that could be perceived as approbation and only make the situation worse. ▶

Bulging eyes, a fearful expression and physical shaking are all signs of a phobic reaction.

You can use the sound of a TV or radio to mask the noise outside, such as thunder or fireworks, that causes fear.

Dogs readily pick up human emotions, so it is important that everyone in the household makes a big effort to stay calm.

Once the noise starts to decrease and your dog begins to relax, go through a few behaviour exercises and reward lavishly a good, correct response. Many behaviourists consider that it is better not to take this latter action **when the sounds start** since it might just serve to draw attention to the fear-evoking stimulus.

If it is necessary to take your dog outside to go to the toilet, be sure to keep it on the lead. Do not leave it unattended even for a minute since in its panic it may well just take off and get lost. Don't leave your dog unattended in the house or car when it has been shown to be concerned about loud noises or flashes of light.

Action To Take On Future Occasions

Adopt a similar procedure to that noted above if it has proved reasonably successful previously but provide the dog in advance with a comfortable bed in a den or bolthole where it can be seen, where it will feel safe and where it can stay until the noise and flashes stop. Generally you will be more successful if you let your dog choose where it wants to go for itself, under a table, in a cupboard or wherever.

If these actions prove unsuccessful consult your vet. In some cases he or she will advise that you use dog-appeasing pheromone (DAP) (see page 25) before your dog becomes agitated and while the sounds continue. In some cases vets will advise that your dog is dosed with anxiolytic drugs (compounds which reduce anxiety) or sedatives before it becomes distressed; sometimes these drugs will be prescribed in combination.

Long-Term Management

As in many cases of inappropriate behaviour, prevention is far better than attempted cure and this is particularly so in the case of firework phobia since dogs may well become excessively fearful and agitated when their owner is not present. In order to be successful, preventive measures need to be taken well in advance of a likely problem situation – pre-planning and purposeful co-operation is fundamental to success. In essence prevention generally calls for a behaviour modification technique called systematic desensitization. This 'tool' is used to break down the dog's anxiety by exposing it to low levels of the stimulus that invokes fear and rewarding the dog when it remains calm. The volume of the stimulus, as a recording, is then increased in intensity little by little until it is tolerated at full strength. Desensitization has to progress at the rate that the dog's responses dictate. Slowly, slowly is the rule. Make every effort not to make a mistake by overdoing the intensity before the dog is ready. CDs of the noise of fireworks and many other fear-inducing sounds are available and these are accompanied by detailed instructions which need to be followed precisely. In the case of need, consult your veterinary surgeon.

Once desenzitisation has proved effective, some behaviourists recommend that a process called counter-conditioning is instigated to teach the dog that the previously phobic sounds in fact herald a rewarding event such as a meal. If you have any doubt about these behaviour modification techniques, it is important to seek advice from your veterinary surgeon or a trained animal behaviourist.

One final word of warning, if a desensitized dog is not exposed occasionally to the actual fear-inducing sound naturally, or by playing the recorded sound on a CD, then its lack of fear could become extinguished.

You can help to desensitize a dog to a sound stimulus that evokes fear by playing a CD of the sound, initially at low volume. The loudness of the recording can then gradually be increased.

PREVENTING INAPPROPRIATE BEHAVIOUR

Introduction

In order to prevent inappropriate behaviour it is essential to know and understand the importance of the information given earlier, in particular with regard to socialization/habituation and basic training. Remember:

- Take time to familiarize your dog to as great a variety of situations, noises and people as possible.
- Train your dog to respond to the basic commands promptly and properly without question.
- Set aside sufficient time to rehearse your dog's response to your chosen commands – that is work as opposed to play.
- Only reward your dog with titbits and/or praise when it has earned them by a proper response. Gratuitous rewards can be very counter-productive and may even make the undesirable behaviour worse.

Taking the actions noted above is fundamental if your dog is to fit comfortably into present-day society. Creating an obedient dog that you can be proud of is indeed a challenge which requires application but which can be both enjoyable and provide a great sense of achievement.

A properly trained dog comes to understand that you and the members of your family are in charge.

Essentially this means that you and your family members must establish yourselves as leaders (see pages 26-7). This can only be achieved by setting firm house rules that everyone must follow consistently. Importantly no one must allow the dog to 'lead' at any time. Privileges, treats and rewards must only be given if they are earned. It is probably best if one member of the family who has the most available time and is most motivated is the person who takes the role of being main trainer/teacher. However, *all the family members* must sing from the same hymn sheet! Prevention is also all about thinking ahead. Training is something that should be ongoing throughout your dog's life but don't forget that your dog's life should be enjoyable and fun, and not just a round of continual schooling.

While thinking about prevention, a few words about dog crates and playpens are relevant. These can play a useful part in preventing inappropriate behaviour because they provide a place to put your dog if problems or temptations to behave badly look likely to occur.

Crates provide a safe haven for your dog, especially when it is very young, if you have to leave it unsupervised for a short time. Furthermore, a crate helps to remove the opportunity for your dog to do any wrong that will subsequently call for corrective procedures. However, never keep your puppy in its crate for extended periods of time and never use confinement in the crate as a form of punishment.

- Crates are made of wire panels that fold down into the size of a suitcase for carrying. They are quick to erect.
- A crate helps with house-training – the door can be shut when the pup is asleep and opened when it wakes up and is taken outside to relieve itself.
- As they are portable, crates can be taken into any room in the house, placed in the garden, or positioned in the back of an estate car.
- Crates are ideal if you visit friends who are not keen on dogs. They can also be used when your dog is ill and needs protection, rest and nursing.
- Play pens are essentially large crates. They form a safe retreat where dogs can see and be seen, in much the same way as a children's play pen is used. They act as a den – a place that offers your dog protection.

Dog crates can be helpful when you are training a puppy. Do take care, however, to introduce the puppy to the crate in a sensitive way and don't use it as a kind of portable prison. It should be a place of refuge, not of unhappy confinement.

If you have a puppy, dog crates are ideal for confining your pet for short periods when you are otherwise occupied and cannot give your dog your full attention, or to help with house-training.

HELPFUL HINTS – DO'S AND DON'T'S

Do choose the right dog for your circumstances – don't rush things or let your heart rule your head when picking a puppy or selecting a dog for adoption.

Do give your dog a name that is short and ensure that everyone uses it regularly, if only to attract the dog's attention and as an introduction to a command.

Do set 'house rules' in respect of where the dog is allowed to go (preferably not upstairs) and what it is not allowed to do. Ensure that everyone observes these rules, *always*.

Don't let puppies do anything you don't want them to do as adults.

Do provide your dog with a comfortable bed placed in a quiet place – respect the dog's space.

Do make a big effort to habituate and socialize your dog when you first have it and as an ongoing task so that it loses its innate fear of common occurrences, sounds and people.

Do play games with your dog to exercise its mind and body. Be careful, however, about playing tug-of-war games, especially with dogs bred for guarding. Make sure that *you* win all the games – if you look like losing, call 'time out' or change the rules.

Do use the leadership exercises described on pages 26-7 twice daily for seven days then once daily for a further seven days, then weekly or monthly as needed to reinforce your leadership role when you first obtain your pet or if your dog tends to get too 'pushy'.

Do give your dog a few extra privileges if it is becoming too submissive as evidenced by lying on its back exposing its abdomen and possibly dribbling urine – but take care not to overdo it.

Do use hand signals as well as verbal commands but be careful not to use them inappropriately.

Do teach your dog that you want it to pay attention by clapping your hands gently and calling its name.

Don't shout at your dog and never punish it if it is slow to come when asked.

Do leave your dog a 'clue' like leaving the radio on and going through a consistent routine when you leave it in the house when you intend to go out.

Don't ever leave your dog in your car with children, no matter how well-behaved it is, and don't leave it in the car with its lead attached to its collar – it could become caught up in the gear lever or brake with potentially disastrous consequences.

Do teach your dog to be well-mannered and not to even *think* about biting, excessive barking, jumping up at people or being disobedient.

Do exercise your dog regularly, and try to vary the walks you go on. Don't make it work at training while on a walk – walking is for fun.

Do think ahead and try to avoid possible conflict and situations where your dog might get it wrong. Better to cross the road if an approaching dog looks like trouble!

Do teach your dog to eat only from its own food bowl and don't let it guard it. Don't give any titbits while eating your own meal at the table.

Don't give your dog more than two or three toys to chew. Never use old shoes and clothes etc. as chew objects. A 15-20cm (6-8in) long hardwood log stripped of its bark and about 7.5-10cm (3-4in) thick makes an ideal chew object.

Don't let your dog go though doors first, lie at the top of the stairs or make you step over it. Your rules, you call the shots!

Do try to make your dog into a happy subordinate, anxious to please but not a slave. Dogs like to know the rules and where they stand.

Dogs appreciate having a comfortable bed that they can call their own, though a four-poster is perhaps carrying indulgence a little far!

All this may sound like a lot of work but the rewards your efforts will bring are well worthwhile. Think what a lift you will get when everyone who meets your dog says 'what a lovely dog, and so well behaved, I wish mine was like that!'

Seeking Additional Help In Respect of Behaviour Problems

With regard to behaviour problems, if you have any doubt about what action to take you should seek advice. The best places to turn to are:

- The breeder– if your dog has been bred by an experienced pedigree dog breeder
- Your veterinary surgeon
- A qualified dog behaviour specialist

It cannot be stressed enough, however, that your aim should always be to prevent inappropriate behaviour. Behaviour specialists can help in a number of difficult cases but their success depends very much on the owner's input and perseverance. In bad cases, particularly those involving aggression, success can be difficult to achieve and unpredictable. Furthermore, be aware that you may need to arrange for several consultations, which can be costly.

Playing games with a dog helps to keep it physically fit and mentally stimulated. It's also fun, and that's what having a dog should be about.

49

MISHAPS AND PROBLEMS ABOUT THE HOUSE AND OUTDOORS

PART

2

CONTENTS

- **INTRODUCTION** Page 52

WHAT IFs?

INDOORS What if my dog...

25 soils my carpets or upholstery either by accident or as a result of illness? Page 52

26 has picked up oil or tar on its coat or paws? Page 54

27 is not fully house-trained and has accidents overnight? Page 55

28 territory marks by urinating against objects in the house? Page 56

29 sheds hair on the furniture, clothing or car upholstery? Page 57

30 needs to be bathed? Page 58

31 needs to be introduced to a new puppy, a new baby, or to a kitten or resident adult cat? Page 59

32 chews chair legs and doors, cushions, shoes and other commonly used items? Page 62

33 will not allow itself to be thoroughly groomed and its ears, eyes, mouth and private parts to be touched and examined? Page 63

34 will not take tablets? Page 64

35 is going to be involved in Christmas celebrations or other festive occasions – what precautions should be taken? Page 65

36 is burnt or scalded accidentally in the kitchen? Page 66

37 seems to be lonely, should I get another dog to keep it company? Page 66

38 has eaten a box of chocolates or a chocolate bar? Page 68

39 has swallowed some human medicines or tablets? Page 68

40 is found unconscious by a source of electricity? Page 69

41 needs to be fed differently because of my changed circumstances – what should it be given and how many daily meals will it need? Page 70

42 is in season and there are male dogs in the house? Page 71

43 makes blood stains on the carpets and furniture when she is on heat? Page 72

44 bites visitors' hands with its very sharp teeth? Page 72

45 licks people's hands and faces? Page 72

46 objects to wearing a collar and fights the lead? Page 73

OUTDOORS **47** passes faeces on the pavement? Page 74

48 kills shrubs by urinating against them? Page 74

49 will not swim? Page 75

50 swallows a stone? Page 75

51 digs in the garden? Page 76

52 passes faeces in the garden – how are they best disposed of? Page 76

53 is stolen? Page 77

54 gets lost and can't find its way home? Page 78

55 gets into a fight with another dog? Page 79

56 is involved in a road traffic accident? Page 81

57 is caught in barbed wire or a thorn hedge? Page 82

58 picks up stones and sand on the beach? Page 82

59 does not behave well in kennels? Page 83

60 is stung by a bee or wasp? Page 83

61 is found unconscious in my car? Page 84

62 makes bleached circles on the lawn where she urinates? Page 84

63 is mated while out on a walk? Page 84

- **YOUR DOG'S SAFETY** Page 86
- **DOG OWNER'S SURVIVAL KITS** Page 87

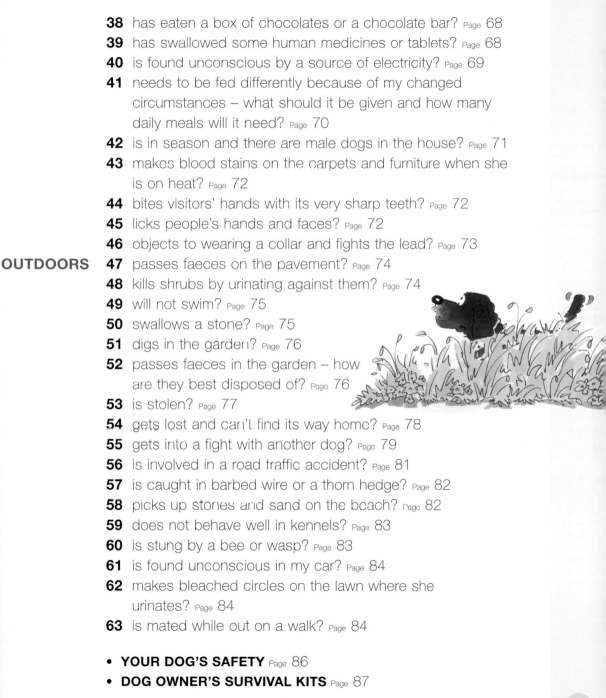

INTRODUCTION

This part of *What If My Dog...?* provides solutions to common problems and mishaps that can occur in respect of dog ownership. If your dog has such a mishap because it is 'off colour', then you can turn a blind eye, but in other cases it is important not to make excuses. It is better to accept that you have a problem and aim to overcome it promptly and to prevent future occurrences.

ABOUT THE HOUSE – ALL DOGS

What if my dog soils my carpets or upholstery either by accident or as a result of illness?

25 In all dog-owning households accidents happen, and frequently soiling with urine, vomit, faeces, grass cuttings, blood, and saliva from drooling dogs can occur. Tar brought into the house from the roads or beach, and oil from under a car or from the garage can also present a problem.

First it is sensible to try to identify why the problem occurred. Was it your fault or your dog's? Or was is simply as a result of illness or advancing old age? Be honest and don't make excuses, unless they are legitimate, and make plans (where relevant) to prevent future occurrences.

Initial Action: Nowadays, a variety of products are available which, it is claimed, can remove both new and old stains virtually whatever their cause. Some are made with pets especially in mind and many combine a stain remover with a biological odour remover, which binds with the odour rather than simply masking it. Such products have the big advantage that they will overcome a dog's natural instinct to return to a place that has been soiled before. Pet healthcare companies also provide disinfectants that are effective against disease-producing bacteria, fungi and viruses. The best quality products are claimed to be non-toxic, non-irritant, non-bleaching and fully biodegradable. It makes a lot of sense to obtain them in advance of any problems and store them safely for use in an emergency so that you can cope with any problem promptly and effectively.

In the case of such accidents, take the following steps:

1 Mop up carefully and thoroughly any fluid with absorbent paper towels or cloths that can be disposed of.

2 Scrape up any solids with an old spatula or similar tool. In some cases it can help to use a product that absorbs the fluid content of any accident by binding the waste material into a dry gel, thus facilitating its removal.

3 Apply a modern stain remover.

4 Apply a non-staining disinfectant if required.

5 Apply a modern odour eliminator.

6 Finally, if necessary use a good deodorizing carpet and upholstery shampoo, dry the surface with a clean cloth and, if time is short, finish the process by using a hair dryer.

Prevention: Useful preventive measures are noted below.

Problem	Action	Further Information
Urine	Make certain that your dog has enough opportunities to go out to be clean and actually does urinate when you take it out. If you suspect illness, consult your vet	See Part 3, 'What if?' no.85
Faeces	Note consistency and colour. If the problem is severe or persistent, seek veterinary advice.	See Part 3, 'What if?' no.81
Vomit	Note the colour, content and the presence of any foreign bodies since veterinary attention may be required. Clean up your dog's coat if it is soiled.	See Part 3, 'What if?' no.65
Blood	Ensure that wounds are securely bandaged. Keep bitches away from items that could be stained when they are on heat. Consider preventing the problem by having your bitch spayed.	See Part 3, 'What if?' nos.82, 86 and 111
Drooling	Dogs with loose flews (jowls) are not able to keep saliva within their mouths. Do not tantalize them with food as that will aggravate the problem. Take precautions if you have visitors – give them a cloth to use or shut your dog away.	See Part 3, 'What if?' no.101

What if my dog has picked up oil or tar on its coat or paws?

26

Oil or tar on your dog's coat

Do not use any inflammable liquid, such as petrol or carbon tetrachloride, on the dog's coat. Cut off as much of the affected hair as possible, and then wash the dog in mild detergent and/or canine shampoo, finishing with a plain water rinse. In the case of tar, it can be helpful first to soften and dilute it with either Swarfega, cooking oil, lard or suntan cream. Work the softening agent well into the affected area and then wash it off with warm water containing a 'soft' detergent such as washing-up liquid. Finally rinse well so that no detergent remains on the skin.

In the case of oil or tar staining, prevention is often the best remedy. Keep an eye on your dog and stop it from wandering unsupervised into the garage or onto newly surfaced roads or tar-polluted beaches.

If your dog has tar on its feet

Clip out the hair and lumps of tar between the pads. Soak the foot in a jug or tall tin containing vegetable oil, or spread Swarfega or lard liberally on the paws, or work in some suntan cream if that is available. When the tar is loosened take great care to prevent your dog licking it off, then wash your dog's feet in warm water containing a 'soft' detergent such as washing-up liquid. Rinse well in plain water so that the detergent does not remain on the skin.

If the tar deposit is very heavy or if a large area is affected, consult a vet at once, as special cleaning measures may be necessary. Some medication may also be needed if it is suspected that significant amounts of tar have been ingested

Tar on soft furnishing or car seats

Rub with Vaseline, sponge with carbon tetrachloride or other organic solvent (your local DIY shop or pet shop may be able to recommend a specific product). Repeat, then wash with detergent and rinse. Always work in decreasing circles from the outside of the stained area. If in doubt, test a small area first or seek professional advice.

Prevention: Do not exercise your dog on beaches contaminated with tar or on roads that have been recently resurfaced or in hot weather when the tarmac has melted. Do not let your dog go into your garage unsupervised and don't let it lie or even crawl under your car.

What if my dog is not fully house-trained and has accidents overnight?

27 Some adult dogs may have the occasional accident overnight but if this is a regular occurrence veterinary attention should be sought to check whether some underlying medical condition is the cause of the problem – see Part 3, 'What if?' nos.69 and 85. Dogs under 4-5 months old cannot be expected to be clean for as long a time as adult dogs.

Possible Causes:

• Illness as noted above.
• Your dog is simply left for too long overnight. Eight to ten hours is as long as a normal, fit dog can take.
• Early morning disturbances, e.g. milkman or paper deliveries. Once your dog is awake, it may feel it needs to be taken out to relieve itself.

• Did your dog actually pass urine when you took it out last thing at night – was it a foul night or were you in a hurry, did you actually see it 'going'?
• Does your dog's basket, bedding or the place where it is left overnight retain the smell or urine or faeces? If so, use a modern disinfectant and odour-removing product; they can be very effective. Avoid the use of bleach or chlorine, they can aggravate smells.

Action: Follow any advice your vet gives in respect of medication, change of diet or frequency of feeding. Train your dog to go to the toilet on command or when it hears the undulating whistle (see Part 1, Toilet training, page 21).

Ensure that the dog's sleeping quarters are disinfected regularly and kept odour-free. Consider letting your dog sleep within the confines of a dog crate (see Part 1, pages 46-7). Finally, don't lie in too long at weekends! If you get up to make a cup of tea, let your dog out while the kettle is boiling and before you go back to bed!

A dog crate prevents your dog from moving around the house at night and relieving itself in an inappropriate place.

What if my dog territory marks by urinating against objects in the house?

28

Unfortunately some entire male dogs and the very occasional bitch will perform this unsavoury act. It should most certainly not be tolerated – do not make excuses but resolve to prevent it.

Possible Causes:

- The trait may be simply a sign that your dog is hypersexed. If this is the case it will probably be showing other signs of this behaviour (see Part 1, 'What if?' no.5).
- Your dog may be trying to establish a dominant role or it may be jealous of the fact that it is not allowed to share your bed. The end of a bed is a very common place for a dog to mark with urine if it adopts this habit.

Action:

- Seek advice from your vet or a trained animal behaviourist and consider having your dog neutered, but note that this is considered to be effective (at least initially) in only about 50 per cent of cases. Modern odour-eliminating products may be helpful but the use of deterrent sprays is questionable since if they contain citronella they may in fact remind the dog where to 'go'. Furthermore some can aggravate the smell of the urine, as indeed can bleach.

Because it is not allowed to share your bed, a jealous dog may territory mark in protest. It is sensible to ban dogs from all the upstairs rooms in the house.

- Use the behaviour control measures noted in Part 1 to establish and reinforce your leadership role.
- Remove temptation and the opportunity. Do make house rules that limit your dog's access to places where it may be inclined to territory mark, such as the ends of beds. Generally it is best to deny dogs access to upstairs rooms.
- Consider setting up a situation which allows you to use 'magic punishment'. Even just saying a very sharp **'No'** with suitable body language, can be very effective if you catch your dog in the very act (see Part 1, page 23).
- Any admonishment *after* the act is of no use whatsoever. Your dog will not associate cause and effect and so such an action could be counter-productive as the dog may perceive it as praise.
- Do not allow your dog contact with a bitch in season since that is likely to exacerbate the situation.

What if my dog sheds hair on the furniture, clothing or car upholstery?

29 Dog hair varies tremendously in the way it adheres to other fabrics. Really long hair can be easier to remove than the short hair shed by Bull Terriers, Dobermanns and similarly coated dogs, which may actually penetrate through the fabric. This can be a particular problem in the case of upholstered car seats. Is changing your car for a model with leather/plastic seats an option?

You may find one of the following aids useful:

- Stroking furniture and clothing with a damp rubber glove on your hand.
- Sticky tape wrapped around the fingers, sticky side outermost, and stroked over fabric pile. Special sticky 'roll-ons' are available which work in the same way.
- Brushing with a damp nailbrush or wiping across the fabric with a damp cloth.

(All these methods roll the hairs together and make them easier to remove.)

Pet hair contains allergens so if you or your family members suffer from allergies or asthma keep your pet off furniture and bedding – you must set house rules when you first obtain your pet. Special attachments for vacuum cleaners are available from pet shops which can make the removal of pet hair more effective. It is also sensible if you have a real and regular problem in this respect to purchase a vacuum cleaner with a turbo nozzle to prevent hair building up on your carpets and upholstery. Consider too selecting a vacuum cleaner with hepa (high efficiency particulate air) filtration as this retains microscopic particles such as house mites, mange mites and bacteria which can otherwise escape back into your home.

Prevention: Groom your dog daily, and especially thoroughly at those times of year when hair is being shed in quantities. If a lot of hair is being shed excessively and unusually or throughout the whole year, have the dog checked for possible underlying skin disease or hormonal upset.

Discuss the dog's diet with your veterinary surgeon to ensure especially that it is getting sufficient B vitamins and unsaturated fatty acids.

Remember to groom your dog regularly, particularly when it is shedding hair in abundance. This stripping tool is designed to thin out a dog's coat.

What if my dog needs to be bathed?

30 Regular bathing of dogs is not a necessity but is usually done by most dog owners two or three times a year. However, the suggestion has recently been made that bathing more regularly will help cement your relationship with your dog and reinforce your status. That apart, your dog may need bathing for medical reasons, because it has started to smell doggy, or has decided to roll in some obnoxious matter!

Large dogs can be bathed quite successfully outside on the ground in good weather. It is sensible before you start to remove your dog's collar if it is made of leather and substitute it with a strong band made of cotton cloth or soft rope. Be sure to use a shampoo especially formulated for dogs and follow the maker's instructions carefully. Soak your dog in plain water first, apply the shampoo, work it well into the coat with your fingers and rinse thoroughly, possibly using a garden hose or watering can. Vigorously towel your dog dry and finish with a hair dryer in breeds with a fine coat. Some vets recommend that a ring of Vaseline should be put around the dog's eyes to keep out soapy water. Alternatively, simply cover your dog's eyes with your hand when shampooing its head.

When bathing a dog, first wet the coat thoroughly with warm, not hot, water. Part the hair to ensure that water has penetrated down to the skin.

Apply the shampoo and work the lather well into the coat. Avoid getting soap in the eyes.

Rinse out the shampoo thoroughly – any soap left in the coat can cause annoying itchiness.

Dry the head first to make the dog feel comfortable, then work along the body and down the legs.

If you have any doubts, seek advice from the breeder or your vet. Be aware that infestation with skin parasites is quite common these days, even in the best-run households. Some very good products are available for use on dogs and around the house, both for the treatment of and, importantly, prevention of flea and other ectoparasite infestations. It pays to seek veterinary advice on this matter and to purchase recommended, products.

What if my dog needs to be introduced to a new puppy, a new baby, or to a kitten or resident adult cat?

31

A New Puppy: Many older dogs take on a new lease of life when a new puppy is brought into the home, provided certain precautions are taken early on.

1 Obtain the puppy as young as possible. At six weeks of age puppies are confident and unafraid, but by eight weeks the puppy may be entering the critical period for sensitivity (see Stages in a Puppy's Development, Part 1, page 22) and may become much more difficult to socialize.

2 Allow the older dog to become accustomed to the puppy while you are present and then allow brief periods of free socialization, *always supervised*.

3 It may be helpful to make an enclosure for the puppy in which it can be left safely for the first few weeks in your home when you are not present. A dog crate or puppy playpen is ideal for the purpose (see Part 1, page 47).

4 Protect the older dog's rights. Do not allow the puppy to make free with its toys, its bed or its food.

5 Make sure the older dog has a full share of attention, and always give a small titbit every time the puppy is fed – older dogs are fed less frequently than puppies.

6 Do not leave the two alone when you are absent until they are at ease with one another – a good indication is if the pair choose to share a bed.

7 Consult your veterinary surgeon about not

Make sure that you are on hand and watching carefully during the early stages of socialization as the resident dog gets to know the new member of the household.

taking the older dog to canine gatherings, or to places where many dogs are exercised, until after the puppy is vaccinated to avoid the possibility of it catching a contagious disease. ▶

A New Baby: A well-kept, healthy dog is unlikely to be a disease risk to a baby so there is no need to bid farewell to a dog which has been a good friend to you and will in the future be a good friend to the child.

Begin to prepare your dog for the new arrival as soon as you know there will be a new baby in your home – don't wait until it arrives!

Teach your dog in advance to be well mannered and obedient; in particular teach it that it must not jump up – *ever*. Prepare your dog for being left in a room on its own more frequently while you are in the house with the baby, but ensure that it still receives sufficient attention. Accustom your dog in advance to carrycots, high chairs and the like. Jealousy of new babies is very uncommon and that is especially so if you plan the introduction of the dog to the baby with care.

TIPS ON INTRODUCING A DOG TO A NEW BABY

1 Let your dog sit beside you when the baby is attended to and talk to it as usual.

2 The baby's cry may be a completely new sound to the dog and may convey a distress message to it; be prepared. Teach your dog that it may look but not touch or jump up at a cot, buggy or pram.

3 If the dog is large and vigorous, make arrangements for it to have sufficient exercise, as walking with a baby in a buggy may not be enough.

4 It can be dangerous to tie a dog to a buggy or pram and leave it unsupervised.

5 Discourage your dog from licking the baby, but let it approach the baby gently – reward good behaviour.

6 Do not let young babies pull the dog's ears and tail.

7 Provide a place into which the dog can retreat away from the baby.

8 *Never* leave your dog alone with the baby in the house, car or garden, especially when the baby is at the crawling stage. Remember that dogs, especially large dogs, can be very vigorous in play.

9 Do not tempt providence by letting the baby play and crawl around the dog's feeding bowl. The dog should be fed separately and any food that is left must be picked up without delay.

10 Take the baby or the dog with you if you have to leave a room even for a few minutes. It is better to be safe than sorry.

11 Teach your dog to recognize the difference between its toys and the baby's.

12 Finally worm your dog with a recommended product, following your vet's advice precisely. See Part 3, page 100.

A New Kitten: Dogs can become very fond of the household cat, even including those that are habitual chasers of unfamiliar cats. Some thoughtful pre-planning before a kitten is introduced into the house can lay the foundations for an easy relationship.

- Bring the kitten into the house in a wire carrying basket so that the dog can become accustomed to the scent and look of the new arrival.
- Give the kitten an escape route so that it can retreat to a safe place out of the dog's reach.
- Put the kitten's litter tray and food where the dog cannot interfere; dogs are attracted to cat faeces.
- Do not leave the two together until you are sure that a mutual respect has developed.
- Most kittens can take very good care of themselves against one dog, but pack action by several dogs is a greater risk.
- Finally, praise the dog and give it delectable food rewards when it behaves properly towards the cat, but admonish it promptly if it chases the cat or objects to its presence.

Puppies and kittens that share a home usually grow up to be good friends, but keep an eye on them during the early stages of companionship as they get to know one another.

Resident Adult Cat: Individual adult animals take additions to the household in a variety of ways, and it is not possible to predict exactly how a resident cat will react. Many cats will be reserved and sulky at first, but most will come to accept the situation and will soon be sharing their bed with the newcomer. Be prepared for the fact that some cats resort to urine-marking indoors to express their displeasure at any change in the household. You may need to seek veterinary advice about how best to proceed in such a case.

Judicious preparations in advance of the new arrival will help ensure that a good relationship between the two animals is established quickly and with minimum hassle.

1 Well ahead of the puppy's arrival, put the cat's litter tray and feeding bowls in a place which the puppy cannot reach.
2 Provide a comfortable sitting area for the cat at a high level.
3 Make sure the cat is not harbouring fleas or ear mites as these are transmissible to dogs.
4 If you have a cat flap in the door, you may wish to keep it closed while the puppy is young and to train the cat to use a window instead.

What if my dog chews chair legs and doors, cushions, shoes and other commonly used items?

32 Puppies have an in-built need to chew, which reaches its peak at 4-6 months of age. The best way to prevent this problem arising is by giving only two or three toys that the dog can chew. It is not a good idea to give an old slipper or a brush, since the dog will not be able to distinguish between that and new shoes or useful brushes. Chew-objects should be unrelated to household items.

This activity calls for the behaviour control methods outlined in Part 1 and responds to instant correction by a thrown object. Set up the situation and as soon as the dog starts to chew the item, admonish it by a well-directed thrown bean bag or similar object. It may help to provide the puppy with an alternative object to chew, such as a hard wood log stripped of its bark, 15-25cm (6-10in) long and of an appropriate diameter for your dog's size, or a proprietary chew-object that does not have sharp edges and that is big enough not to be swallowed whole. Every time you see the dog about to attack the furniture, direct its attention to its own chews.

No-one wants to see their precious furnishings chewed to shreds. 'Magic punishment' is an effective way of deterring a dog that is about to chew something inappropriate.

If all this fails, consider confinement of your puppy in a dog crate for short periods when your attention is elsewhere.

Finally, anti-chew sprays can be bought at pet shops – the most expensive ones are quite effective but the cheaper varieties are not. However, it is much better in the long term not to rely on deterrent sprays but to train the dog that chewing does not please you and that **not** chewing is more rewarding.

What if my dog will not allow itself to be thoroughly groomed and its ears, eyes, mouth and private parts to be touched and examined?

33

Puppies: Puppies should be made to submit to grooming and having various parts of their anatomy examined from the first day in their new home even if they have very little coat at that time.

Either groom your puppy on the floor or put something on a table top that will not slip about and which the dog's feet can grip. An old piece of rubber-backed carpet is ideal. This has the added advantage that you will not have to stoop and so grooming will become more pleasant for you and the dog and less of a chore.

Grooming your dog regularly will make it unnecessary to have long and painful disentangling sessions. The correct grooming tools make the process easier. Consult the dog's breeder, if you have a pedigree dog, or ask for advice at a pet shop or grooming parlour so that you can obtain the most suitable tools for your dog's breed and coat.

Remember to praise the dog for good behaviour, possibly by giving a titbit and admonish it effectively if it growls or makes a fuss. If the dog tends to misbehave or even snap in such situations, go through the dominance/ leadership exercises described in Part 1, pages 26-7.

Adult Dogs: This behaviour is most commonly exhibited when your dog is trying to become more dominant and exert its authority over you. However, in some cases it can be the result of the grooming process causing pain, e.g. if the dog has a wound, an ear problem or arthritis. If you think this could be the case, especially if the difficulty has just arisen in a normally well-behaved dog, try to locate the cause, and if necessary seeking veterinary help.

Regular grooming will go a long way to help cement your relationship with your pet. It also provides you with an ideal opportunity to feel over your dog's body for any lumps, bumps or abrasions that might need veterinary attention.

Remedial Action:
- Treat any underlying medical cause.
- Reinstate your leadership role as noted in Part 1, pages 26-7.
- Start by being less vigorous about grooming, having first checked that your grooming tools are not too sharp or abrasive. Concentrate first on grooming those areas that are more acceptable to your dog, like its back for example, and progress *slowly* to more sensitive areas. Try to ensure that you don't have failures on the way; if you do, go back a step or two and start again.

63

What if my dog will not take tablets?

34 It is important to practise tablet-giving from the time you first obtain a puppy. Put small vitamin/mineral supplement tablets deliberately down its throat occasionally, even though they are actually palatable enough for the puppy to eat them. This will help you to acquire the skill of dosing your dog which could be invaluable in the future.

Some owners get flustered when they have to administer a pill to their dogs. There is no need – it's really quite simple if you follow the step-by-step method described here.

Actual medicinal tablets are much more satisfactory given whole, than crushed on food or disguised in other ways. Here is how to administer tablets to a reluctant dog.

1 Stand in front of your dog, but slightly on its right-hand side, while its left side is pressed against a wall or solid object by a willing assistant.

2 Cup your left hand* around the dog's muzzle and open the top jaw by pressing its lips into the gap just in front of the carnassial tooth and behind the large canine tooth on each side of the dog's mouth in the upper jaw. The lips should cover the upper carnassial teeth on each side. To do this, use your thumb on one side of the jaw and your first and second fingers on the other – they will be protected from being bitten by the dog's lips.

3 Hold the tablet between the thumb and the first and second fingers of your right hand, still holding the dog's muzzle as noted above. Open the mouth wide by tipping the dog's head up and back and by pressing down on the lower incisors with the third finger of your right hand. Pop the pill onto the centre of the tongue as far back in the mouth as you can. If the tablet is put in the right place, the dog will have no option but to swallow it.

4 Hold the mouth closed until the dog swallows the pill, then praise the dog and release it. Job done!

* The method described relates to right-handed people – if you are left-handed use the opposite hand to that noted.

What if my dog is going to be involved in Christmas celebrations or other festive occasions – what precautions should be taken?

It's natural to want your dog to share in Christmas festivities and to give it some extra treats from the meal, but do be careful with chicken and turkey leftovers. Any stray bones may be crunched up and cause serious problems in the dog's intestines.

35 Events like Christmas and the New Year, or birthday parties, are times which should be enjoyed by people and pets. Take these precautions to ensure they are not spoiled by problems with your dog:

- If you give your dog any remains of a chicken or turkey, ensure they do not contain any bones. Sharp bones or flakes of bone can penetrate the digestive tract. Crunched-up bones may cause serious constipation.
- Be careful not to leave silver foil, wrapping paper, small toys or gifts from crackers lying around. They may be swallowed and become lodged in the intestines requiring surgical removal.
- Ensure elastic bands are disposed of carefully and promptly, as they can become attached to a pet's tongue or be placed on a leg or tail by children, with disastrous results.
- Make sure that electric wires to Christmas tree lights are correctly installed and are connected to a properly fused plug.
- Don't go out and leave pets in a room with table lights and tree lights switched on.
- Don't feed your pet too many titbits or large quantities of food it isn't used to.
- Do not give your dog pieces of chocolate as a treat or leave chocolates where dogs can pick them up. Chocolate contains theobromine which is toxic to dogs even in small amounts. See 'What if?' no.38.
- Do take precautions if your dog has a phobia about loud noises and flashes of light. See Part 1, 'What if?' no.24.

What if my dog is burnt or scalded accidentally in the kitchen?

36

Initial Action:
- Gently clip off the hair over the affected area; the injury may be more extensive than you think.
- Apply cold water compresses, cold running water, or ice cubes to reduce the inflammation, to limit damage to tissues and to help relieve the pain.
- Don't be surprised if your dog resents you touching the area.
- If the scald has been caused by a water-soluble fluid, e.g. boiling milk or jam, cold water will remove them.
- However, if hot oil or fat are involved, these must be removed promptly to prevent them congealing on the coat and sealing in the heat. In such cases use a mild detergent first to loosen the fat and then apply cold water.
- Assess the depth of the burn or scald; first and second degree burns (superficial) penetrate no deeper than the skin surface, third degree burns penetrate through the thickness of the skin into the tissue beneath.

Subsequent Action: If you consider that you have to deal with anything more than a second degree burn, *seek veterinary assistance as an emergency*. Your dog may need specialized treatment to prevent subsequent infection and possibly to overcome the effects of shock. If the injury is less severe, in most cases all that is required is to keep the area clean and to apply a simple antiseptic cream once or twice daily. If pain persists, however, or if you have any doubts, do seek veterinary help sooner rather than later.

What if my dog seems to be lonely, should I get another dog to keep it company?

37

Some prospective dog owners consider obtaining two dogs rather than just one because they believe that they will be happier together. Many vets are of the opinion, however, that generally this is not a good option for the following reasons. First, dogs are very content to have just the attention of people as long as they are given the necessary time by their owners. Secondly, it is not possible to give as much attention to each individual if you have more than one dog. Thirdly, it is difficult to avoid favouring one dog more than the other and this can lead to jealousy between them with constant bickering and occasionally serious fighting. See also preventing jealousy between dogs, Part 1, 'What if?' no.6.

Finally, one word of caution should be noted.

Generally where there are two dogs together in one household, they will sort out a 'pecking order' between themselves with you as their pack leader. All may be well when you are present but in your absence things may go wrong. Many of the unfortunate serious attacks on children, and other dogs and cats have been caused by a pack of such dogs (just two is enough) running amok in the absence of the owner or when not under proper control.

Overall it is probably better in most situations to settle for just one dog, determining to give it your full, undivided attention and

If you favour one dog more than the other, you may set up a situation where feelings of jealousy eventually boil over and result in an outbreak of quite serious fighting.

If a second dog comes to share your home, be prepared for some initial competition as the two dogs establish a domestic 'pecking order'.

bringing it up by the method described in Part 1 to be a well-mannered, obedient dog. If you have a really good rapport and a firm relationship with your present dog, don't risk destroying that by getting another – it's too important to both you and your dog.

67

What if my dog has eaten a box of chocolates or a chocolate bar?

38 Chocolate contains theobromine which can be toxic to dogs causing stimulation of the brain, heart and respiratory system. The amount of theobromine in different chocolate products varies. Milk chocolate contains the least; plain chocolate about six times as much, cocoa powder more still and cocoa shell garden mulch the most. In practical terms for a 10kg (22lb) dog, for example a Dachshund or a West Highland Terrier, the following amounts could prove fatal: two and a half large bars of milk chocolate, three-quarters of a small bar of plain chocolate, one-quarter of a 250g tin of cocoa powder or just four tablespoons of cocoa shell garden mulch.

Don't do it! For us a box of chocolates is one of life's treats; for dogs chocolates are one of life's hazards, and potentially fatal to them.

This means that if your dog comes to you smelling of chocolate, observe it closely for the next four to 24 hours. Should it show signs of vomiting, excessive thirst, excitability, salivation or look unsteady on its feet, *seek veterinary help without delay*. There is no specific antidote but supportive treatment can help.

In the main prevention is better then cure. If you must give chocolate to your dog, use milk and not plain chocolate. Better still give especially formulated doggy choc drops, which don't actually contain any chocolate!

Dog owners should use garden composts which don't contain cocoa shell mulch and should keep all products containing chocolate securely shut away.

What if my dog has swallowed some human medicines or tablets?

39 **Initial Action:** Gather together as much evidence as you can in respect of what exactly your dog has eaten and, if possible, how much. Take your dog to your veterinary surgeon *at once* and be prepared to give the vet a full history of the occurrence and show him any relevant medicinal packaging and a sample of any vomit your dog may have produced.

Subsequent Action: Follow your vet's advice precisely and resolve to keep any medicines you have in the house, or for that matter *any* poisonous substances, in well-sealed containers that are shut well away where your dog cannot get at them.

What if my dog is found unconscious by a source of electricity?

40

Initial Action: Switch off the electricity. If this is not possible, *do not touch the dog with your hands* but move it away from the power source with a wooden broom. Pull your dog's tongue forward to ensure that its airway is clear. Lie it down on its side and press rhythmically and intermittently on its chest at about five-second intervals to induce breathing. If that fails then administer mouth to nose resuscitation (see also Part 3, 'What if?' no.76). If possible, keep these actions going while you transport your dog to a veterinary surgery. Use your mobile phone to alert your vet of the circumstances and of your imminent arrival.

1 *Use a broom or a wooden pole to move the dog safely away from the source of electricity.*

2 *Pull its tongue forward in the mouth and pull its head straight to ensure that the airway is clear.*

4 *If that doesn't work, blow gently into the dog's nose to inflate the lungs, and repeat at regular intervals of around 4 to 6 seconds.*

3 *Press rhythmically on the dog's chest at about five-second intervals to attempt to restart breathing.*

Subsequent Action: Follow your vet's advice precisely and resolve to check that all your electrical appliances are properly connected and kept as far as possible out of your dog's reach.

What if my dog needs to be fed differently because of my changed circumstances – what should it be given and how many daily meals will it need?

41

Dogs can thrive on a great variety of food including:
- Commercially produced complete food, presented in cans, pouches or as dry food.
- Home-made meals containing meat, cereals and our leftovers.
- Commercial mixer (biscuit meal) for mixing and feeding with either of the above foods.

Usually most vets recommend the use of commercially produced complete dog food from reputable companies since they contain all the nutrients dogs need in the correct balance. They offer good palatability, digestibility and a suitable energy density (the dog can get enough energy without over-filling its stomach). Such diets also offer consistency, safety and convenience. However, rather than throw away good leftover human food, like the remains of a stew, uneaten scrambled eggs or fish (look out for bones!), it does make sense to give small amounts of such leftovers *as a supplement*. Such additions, if made, should not make up more than ten per cent of the total daily intake of food, so that the balance of nutrients is not disturbed. Dogs that have had their diet supplemented in this way have the advantage that there is always a source of food that they will eat readily in any unexpected circumstance – but don't overdo it.

The majority of vets consider that the use of complete dry foods offers the best option for most dog owners. This type of food is convenient, it can be easily stored and the exact amount required can be measured simply so that food is not wasted. Dry food can be put down for the dog to eat when it is left on its own without the risk of it going off or attracting flies, and it is convenient to use if the dog is taken on holiday or for a lengthy day trip. By contrast, any canned food or food presented in a sachet that is not used at the time inevitably will need to be kept in a refrigerator.

However, despite the comments made above, it has to be accepted that the feeding of dogs does come down to personal preference – there are no hard and fast rules or absolute rights and wrongs. Furthermore new products are continually being offered and their pros and cons will need to be assessed by you, if necessary in consultation with your veterinary surgeon,

Vets generally recommend feeding commercially produced complete dog foods. They are available in specially made formulations for dogs of all ages.

a practice nurse or the supplier or manufacturer. Reputable companies offer a good service in this respect.

Whatever method you adopt, it is important to feed good quality food and preferably a recognized brand. Always read the directions on the label and feed the diet in accordance with the instructions. One final word of warning, it is not advisable to feed cow's milk to young puppies and only in moderation, if at all, to adult dogs, since it can cause digestive upsets.

If you have any doubts about how to feed your dog, seek advice from the breeder, if you have a pedigree dog, or from your vet or the veterinary nurse.

BITCHES

What if my bitch is in season and there are male dogs in the house?

42 Consult a veterinary surgeon about the prevention of heat on a temporary or permanent basis – spaying or chemical methods are available (see Part 3, 'What if?' no.115). Castration of the male (see Part 3, 'What if?' no.102 and Part 1, 'What if?' no.5) may be effective but he may still show some mating behaviour. In these cases castration is only likely to be effective in 70 per cent of cases at best.

If you think your bitch may have escaped and been mismated, see Part 3, 'What if?' no.112. If your bitch is found to be pregnant unexpectedly, see Part 3, 'What if?' no.113.

What if my bitch makes blood stains on the carpets and furniture when she is on heat?

43 The amount of blood-stained discharge when in season varies from bitch to bitch. Some bitches will lick themselves much more frequently when in season and so cause little problem; other bitches are not so meticulous.

Immediate Action: See 'What if?' no.25.

Prevention:

- Confine the bitch to easily-washed areas while she is in season.
- Cover furniture with old sheets of similar cotton material.
- If the bitch is not to be bred from, consider eliminating the nuisance of heat by having your bitch spayed. See Heat Control, Part 3, 'What if?' no.115.

PUPPIES

What if my puppy bites visitors' hands with its very sharp teeth?

44 Many people like to offer a puppy their finger to bite, but when the habit is established, elderly people with prominent veins and fragile skin may not enjoy the situation.

Action: The command **'No!'** accompanied by an immediate sharp tap on the muzzle should deter the puppy. Give the dog its own chew-object in exchange. Ask other members of the family and visitors not to encourage hand-biting. See also Part 1, 'What if?' no.2.

What if my puppy licks people's hands and faces?

45 People are very much divided concerning the acceptability of this habit. Some like it because they consider it shows that the puppy approves of them and loves them. Others consider it unacceptable hygienically and fear that the puppy might transmit some infection to them. See also Part 1, 'What if?' no.18.

In general it is better to discourage this behaviour by reinforcing your leadership role (see Part 1, page 26) and by uttering a sharply given command **'No'** together with mild punishment (a light tap on the puppy's nose) *as the act is being committed*. Take prompt action to avoid the puppy having the chance to reach people's faces and ask visitors not to encourage your puppy to behave in this way.

On balance, it is better not to allow a young dog to leap up and lick people's faces even if you personally enjoy the display of affection. Visitors may find it offensive and young children can be bowled over in the process.

What if my puppy objects to wearing a collar and fights the lead?

46 When you first get your puppy, buy a small, soft collar and put it on for short periods under supervision. If the puppy looks agitated after a little while, take it off before it starts getting really worried and scratching continually at the collar. Repeat the exercise later and give praise for longer periods of tolerance. As the puppy grows, buy progressively bigger collars (you may need to buy two or three of increasing size) that fit comfortably and that are not so loose that they can become lost or snag on protruding objects. Some specific types of collars suit certain breeds best, the breeder should be able to advise. Choke chains look good on bigger, short coated breeds, like Dobermanns for example, but like slip collars, they should only be used on older puppies and then with caution and restraint. Misuse can cause serious injury.

The new style of head or face collars are especially useful for dogs that tend to pull on the lead, or lunge at other dogs, because the control point is under the chin rather than round the neck. The new control walking harnesses are also useful for dogs that have neck injuries, taking pressure away from the neck region. They have also been used with success with larger breeds that do not take well to head collars, since they discourage pulling on the lead by exerting pressure under the armpits. The old fashioned harnesses are rather outdated and have no place with big strong dogs since the owner has virtually no control; furthermore they can interfere with the dog's natural gait.

See also Part 1, Basic Training, Heel, page 20.

If the problem has already become established, it may help to try the following strategy. Put the collar and lead on immediately before feeding the dog. Put the food on the far side of the room where the dog can see it. Hold the lead while the dog goes over to the food and let it trail while the dog is eating. Repeat at several meal times so that the dog is diverted from fighting the collar and associates its collar and lead with something pleasant.

Body harnesses (above) and face collars (right) are both designed to teach a dog to walk obediently to heel by making the action of pulling on the lead uncomfortable for the dog.

OUTDOORS – ALL DOGS

What if my dog passes faeces on the pavement?

47 Anti-fouling laws are here to stay and must be enforced as a social necessity. Owners must recognize the need to clear dog faeces away in parks and on pavements, and local authorities should co-operate by providing plenty of disposal bins.

Above right: 'Poop scoops' like this make the collection and disposal of dog faeces quite straightforward. Responsible owners should not allow their dogs to foul public spaces.

Immediate Action: Always carry a plastic bag or one of the scooping gadgets available from pet shops and veterinary surgeries when exercising your dog in a public place. Do not be too proud or self-conscious to pick up after your own dog! This action is now universally accepted.

Prevention: Give your dog the opportunity to pass faeces in an acceptable place before taking it for walks on the pavement, around parks or playing fields, or on beaches.

What if my male dog kills shrubs by urinating against them?

48 Most male dogs, including those which are castrated, establish marking posts around their territory on which they urinate regularly. Low-growing conifers, especially junipers, seem to be favourite sites, but any plant will do!

Immediate Action: Douse the plant with quantities of water which may save it from urine burn.

Prevention: Leave the dead shrub in position rather than replacing with another or put a wooden post in its place. Close observation of the dog and the command **'No!'** as it approaches the area may induce the dog to alter its site. This is an ideal situation for correction by a thrown object, having first set the scene and waited in hiding for the dog to offend. (See Part 1, Magic Punishment, page 23.)

What if my dog will not swim?

49 Most dogs can swim if they have to but many find it difficult to climb out of pools with vertical sides, so great care must be taken with garden swimming pools, especially when they are partially covered. Tragedies have occurred. Many dogs are afraid of waves thundering on a beach and are reluctant to jump into a river from a steep bank.

Choose a lake with a gentle slope into the water and play with the dog in the shallows until it gains confidence. Teaching your dog to swim could prevent an unfortunate accident later on.

What if my dog swallows a stone?

50 Many puppies are addicted to eating gravel. It may do no harm but should be prevented as far as possible.

If you see your dog swallow a large stone, however, take it to the veterinary surgeon at once, as it may be possible to induce the dog to vomit the stone. This will have to be done quickly; once in the intestine, the stone may cause an obstruction which can only be relieved surgically.

It is never a good idea to throw stones for dogs. If a dog shows an inclination to eat gravel or stones on the beach, it should be sharply admonished, possibly by using a suitable thrown object. Prevention is far better than cure.

What if my dog digs in the garden?

51

Digging is a natural behaviour for most dogs, but is especially strong in terriers and Dachshunds. Dogs may dig holes in order to:

- bury bones and toys (a natural instinct for secreting prizes).
- catch moles and rodents burrowing below the surface.
- create a cool hollow in which to lie during hot weather.
- escape into the wider world, possibly with a bitch in mind.

Prevention Methods: Remove the opportunity for your dog to dig in places that are unacceptable by using fencing or covering areas with concrete slabs or stones. Keep an eye on your dog when it is loose in the garden and try to catch it in the act so that you can admonish it promptly. 'Magic punishment' involving a thrown object can be very effective in such a situation.

What if my dog passes faeces in the garden – how are they best disposed of?

52

Small amounts of dog faeces picked up from the garden or recovered from the ground when out walking with the dog may be put into the sewage system via the WC.

Special dog WCs can be bought. They consist of a plastic dustbin-like container which is sunk into the ground and charged with a disinfectant-type fluid which liquidizes faeces deposited in it. The contents may be emptied into a pit dug on waste ground, or emptied into the sewage system.

The faeces of adult dogs may be put onto compost heaps, but if there is any chance that the faeces may contain roundworm or tapeworm eggs, this disposal method is unsuitable as the compost heap will not attain enough heat to kill the eggs.

Faeces from puppies are best rolled in plenty of newspaper and burnt if possible or taken to an amenity tip to be buried with other household rubbish. This is because, unless the puppy has recently been wormed with a modern wormer, its faeces are very likely to contain eggs of the roundworm *Toxocara canis* which can infect people. See Part 3, pages 100-1.

What if my dog is stolen?

53 There is a growing risk that pedigree puppies and adult dogs may be stolen from cars, and even from their gardens or when tied up outside shops. Most of the specialist canine insurance companies offer cover for theft of a dog, together with reimbursement of some of the costs of advertising and offering a reward, but this is of little consolation to a bereft owner.

If you cannot find your dog, first check with the police, the local veterinary surgeries and rescue kennels that the dog has not been taken to one of these places by someone who found the dog on the street. Check again every other day. In some areas a dog Helpline may be in operation.

Where it is certain that a dog has been stolen, the best tactic is to have a leaflet printed showing a photograph and description of the dog. Circulate it as widely as possible and display it in shops that offer that facility. Also contact the canine press so that breeders may be on the alert for a new dog coming into their area possibly in suspicious circumstances.

It's convenient to secure your dog to a fence or lamp-post if you have to pop inside a shop for a moment, but sadly some owners emerge to discover that the dog has gone.

Offer a reward, but note that it is illegal to state that 'no questions will be asked if the animal is returned', as this constitutes conniving with the thieves.

Do not give up hope of seeing your dog again, as it may escape or be turned loose to make its way home several days or even weeks after the theft.

What if my dog gets lost and can't find its way home?

54 In the UK all dogs must, by law, wear a name tag, so that ownership can be traced. Remember to alter the tag appropriately if you are on holiday. More and more dog owners are having an electronic identity chip implanted in the neck of their dog, or having it tattooed, so that their pets can more readily be identified. Microchips are the state-of-the-art method of permanent dog identification.

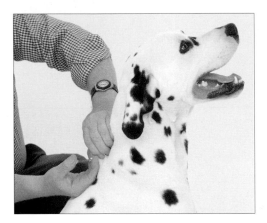

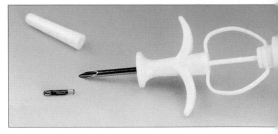

A Dalmatian having a tracer microchip implanted under the skin of its neck. Details of the chip and the implanter are shown above right.

If your dog gets lost on a walk, turn around and retrace the route by which you came, all the way back to your starting point. The dog thus has two opportunities to pick up your scent, and can also follow its own tracks.

A dog will often return to the place where you parked the car. Many dogs tend to remain quite close to the place at which they were lost, especially when in woodland.

Immediate Action: Visit the place at which the dog was last seen early in the morning and at dusk each day, and be prepared to wait quietly for some time. Walk about slowly as dogs see moving figures more easily than those which are standing still. Call your dog's name repeatedly. It may help to take a familiar canine companion to the scene – a bitch in season can work wonders for attracting a male.

Report the loss separately to every police station over a wide area, and to local veterinary surgeons, in case the dog has been found injured, and to rescue kennels and breed rescue societies.

Alert a selection of people to look out for the dog, but beware of having too many over-enthusiastic searchers, especially children, who may frighten the dog even further away.

HOW DO I FIND MY WAY HOME?

Make sure that your dog wears a durable name tag and that your telephone number is clearly engraved on one side so that you can be alerted if the dog should be found after going missing.

Subsequent Action: Make sure your dog always wears a name tag on which your name, address and telephone number are readable and remember to keep it up to date. Old tags can become so blurred as to be useless.

For use on holiday, buy a cylinder name and address holder into which a slip of paper can be put bearing your holiday address.

Most canine veterinary insurance policies give some cover towards the costs of advertising and reward for a missing dog.

What if my dog gets into a fight with another dog?

55
Your dog will soon get a bad reputation if it even threatens other dogs when they meet. It is also a major cause for concern and embarrassment for owners. Don't make excuses for your dog. Accept that it has a problem and resolve to do something about it.

Fighting to establish supremacy is a natural behaviour in dogs. When a dog has this tendency, strong leadership status must be established by the owner – see Part 1. The dog should not be taken out by people who cannot control it.

Avoidance strategy should also be employed by not taking the dog into public parks etc. and by taking it out at quiet times of day. It is important to train dogs to respect the word **'Leave'**. The dog should learn that to obey the word **'Leave'** brings rewards. If another dog approaches, start telling your dog to **'Leave'** before a situation develops. Use the command **'Sit'** and reward your dog lavishly when it responds properly and promptly.

Once a dog is in a fight, breaking up the conflict is a matter of improvization. Fighting dogs are usually oblivious to the pain of being

79

hit with sticks or leads, and dragging them apart is useless. The owner of the larger dog would do well to walk away, calling the dog encouragingly to follow in a normal manner. It is best neither to admonish nor praise either dog since these actions could exacerbate the situation. Surprise is a good friend on these occasions. Quantities of water administered via a hose or bucket, a diversionary noise, even an unfamiliar voice shouting, may cause the dogs to break out of curiosity. Shouting by

Don't assume that a small dog will always back away from confronting a larger dog. As many a Chihuahua owner will confirm, the fighting spirit in a dog is not directly proportional to its physical size.

the owners often seems to spur the dogs on to fight harder.

If one or both dogs are wearing collars, the collar may be twisted by hand or with a stick to momentarily cut off their air supply and allow control of the dog to be regained. But remember the risk of being bitten in the mêlée can be quite high; it may be more prudent to walk away calling the dog to follow. Dogs seldom fight to the death and usually one will surrender. Never pull one of the participants up by the collar so that it stands on its hind legs, exposing its underbelly to the opponent. When the dogs have parted, get control immediately and remove them at once out of range of each other or they will resume the fight at the first opportunity.

Talk to the other owner about the problem but avoid taking an aggressive, provocative stance. If necessary both dogs should be taken for a veterinary examination since any wounds may need dressing, and antibiotic cover may be required, especially in respect of puncture wounds. It could help to discuss with your vet whether castrating your dog could be beneficial. To help avoid a repetition of the problem, see also Part 1, 'What if?' no.10.

What if my dog is involved in a road traffic accident?

56 This can be an extremely traumatic occurrence which can to some extent be minimized by thinking ahead about the actions that should be taken.
Your immediate response should be to:

- Hold up the traffic.
- Restrain the dog, perhaps by throwing a coat over its head, while you collect your thoughts and gather what you need for first-aid treatment.
- Loop a restraining lead over the dog's head. Even a badly injured dog may run away from the scene, complicating your efforts to help. Protect yourself by whatever means possible, e.g. thick gloves. Put on an emergency muzzle *unless the dog is having trouble with breathing*.
- Gently move the dog to the roadside, if necessary by lifting it onto a blanket or coat and sliding it along.

Provided the dog is not having trouble breathing, it is a sensible precaution to use a length of cord to fashion a temporary muzzle. The ends are passed around the neck and tied behind the ears.

- If blood is being lost, apply a large pad to the wound with firm pressure, adding more pads if the blood seeps through. Consider controlling bleeding by using a tourniquet but only if blood is actually spouting from the wound. If that is not the case, pressure bandages usually work and are safer (see Part 3, 'What if?' no.95).
- Locate a veterinary surgery to which the dog can be taken. If fractures are suspected, transport the dog on a board.
- Keep the dog lightly covered and warm during transport to the surgery.

1 *A coat and two poles can furnish an emergency stretcher.*

2 *The coat is fastened and the poles pass through the sleeves.*

3 *The dog can then be lifted gently onto the improvised carrier.*

What if my dog is caught in barbed wire or a thorn hedge?

57 Pause long enough to protect yourself with strong gloves and consider throwing a coat over your dog's head – it may be uncharacteristically aggressive as a result of pain. Put your dog on its lead so that it cannot run away and proceed to cut it free, while talking to it and giving reassurance. If you do not have any cutters to hand, try to enlist the help of a passer-by who may be able to fetch a sharp knife, scissors, pliers or other cutting tool while you stay with the dog to keep it calm. Or telephone for assistance using a mobile phone. Don't simply try to pull the dog free by hand – you will only make the situation worse.

Don't attempt to remove the bits of brambles or wire that are embedded in your dog's skin and/or flesh until you have freed it, then proceed slowly and carefully without the use of force. If that proves difficult, take your dog to the veterinary surgery. Otherwise clean the wounds, clipping away hair if necessary and apply some liquid antiseptic, such as TCP. Usually wounds of this nature heal quite quickly but veterinary attention including the possibility of the administration of antibiotics will be needed if there are extensive lacerations or deep puncture wounds.

What if my dog picks up stones and sand on the beach?

58 A dog can consume quite large quantities of sand while playing ball on the beach. If this occurs or if you see your dog eating something unidentified on the beach, a spoonful of liquid paraffin administered that night and the next morning can help prevent problems (see Part 3 'What if?' no.83 for dosage). If your dog subsequently refuses to eat, has diarrhoea or any other sign of illness, seek veterinary attention. See also Part 3 'What if?' no.66.

Never ever throw stones for your dog to retrieve on the beach – teeth can all too easily be damaged in this way. Similarly it is important to stop your dog drinking sea water, which can make it sick, by using the behaviour control measures noted in Part 1, i.e. a sharp command of **'No'** coupled with a learned command like **'Sit'** which can then be rewarded.

Don't encourage your dog to chase stones on a beach – if you do, its teeth may suffer.

What if my dog does not behave well in kennels?

59

This situation is unlikely to occur if you have followed the advice given in Part 1. Leaving your dog's own bedding and a favourite toy or chew-object with the kennel owner can help your dog to settle in. Leaving young puppies in kennels for just a night or two when they are about 5-6 months old will help to prevent problems later when you go on a longer holiday. Your dog will learn by experience that kennelling is not for life and that you will be returning to be reunited.

What if my dog is stung by a bee or wasp?

60

Insect bites and stings can result in rapid swelling and, in severe cases, a dangerous allergic reaction may ensue. Rapid first-aid measures are called for. For advice on the best course of action to adopt to deal with bites and stings, see Part 3, 'What if?' no.94.

What if my dog is found unconscious in my car?

61 If dogs are left in a car in the summer, they *must* be given adequate ventilation and be left in the shade. If proper precautions are not taken to protect the dog from the effects of the sun in an enclosed vehicle, it can develop heat stroke which may ultimately lead to unconsciousness and even death. For advice on how to deal with a dog that has suffered a heat-induced collapse, see Heat Stroke, Part 3, 'What if?' no.76.

BITCHES

What if my bitch makes bleached circles on the lawn where she urinates?

62 **Immediate Action:** The grass can be prevented from turning yellow by pouring two or three gallons of water onto the affected area immediately the urine has been passed.

Prevention: With patience bitches can be trained to use a concrete, gravel or soil area. Prevention is not possible if a bitch is habitually allowed to urinate on the lawn.

OH NO! NOT THE GRAVEL!!

What if my in-season bitch is mated while out on a walk?

63 **Immediate Action: The mating process**
Because the male dog has a small bone in its penis, penetration is achieved without full erection. Once inside the vagina, the glandular part of the penis becomes engorged with blood and this is accompanied by strong thrusting movements, resulting in the ejaculation of the

first part of the semen, which contains few, if any, spermatozoa. Once pelvic thrusting ends, the male will dismount, with its penis still within the bitch's vagina.

By turning and lifting one hind leg over the bitch the dog will end up 'tied' to her, tail to tail, locked by the engorged penis which, together with the contractions of the vaginal muscles after coitus, makes separation difficult. During the 'tie' ejaculation of seminal fluid continues; this second part is rich in spermatozoa.

No attempt should be made to separate animals locked in this way since the dog will be released in good time. Buckets of cold water thrown over the animals simply wet them and do little or nothing to speed up the separation process.

The tie can last anything from five minutes to one hour (average 20 minutes) and during this time, the bitch and the dog may drag each other around. Although possibly disconcerting to the uninitiated, this behaviour is not usually a cause for concern and seldom results in damage to either animal.

If you discover your bitch in the 'tied' position after a male dog has unexpectedly mounted her, don't panic and try to separate the dogs by force. No good will come of this. Be patient and wait for the tie to break naturally. Then seek prompt veterinary advice to avert the risk of pregnancy.

However, it is sensible to remain on hand and to be prepared to restrain the dog and the bitch if the movement is excessive. The tie finally breaks quite spontaneously and some of the seminal fluid will be seen draining from the bitch's vulva.

Subsequent Action: See the advice about Mismating, Part 3, 'What if?' no.112.

Prevention: See Heat control in bitches, Part 3, 'What if?' no.115.

YOUR DOG'S SAFETY

Dogs, like people, can all too easily have accidents which can cause injury or even death. If you follow the tips noted below, such risks will be kept to a minimum. As a diligent owner you should always be aware of, and alert to, possible dangers for your dog and take steps to ensure its safety. Think ahead and look out for potential hazards.

SAFETY TIPS

INDOORS

- Protect open fires with a fire guard.
- Ensure that electrical leads are out of reach and that all electrical appliances are properly earthed and are connected to a fused plug.
- Keep all cleaning products including detergents and disinfectants out of reach and preferably in secure cupboards.
- Discard rubber bands properly and promptly. They can easily get wrapped around a dog's tongue, paw or tail with disastrous consequences.
- Kitchens are best kept out of bounds when cooking since hot liquids can easily be spilt.
- Give specially merchandised dog chews rather than bones of any type which may be crunched up into splinters.
- Make sure that all larger, and valuable, ornaments are out of reach and placed securely so that they will not fall.
- Some house plants can be poisonous or irritating to dogs and should be kept out of reach. If in doubt, consult a good plant manual or check at a garden centre.
- Never give chocolates as a treat, even small quantities can cause illness or even death.

- Keep rubbish bins firmly shut.
- Make sure that dog toys are not too hard, nor too soft, and that they don't have sharp edges or are small enough to be swallowed whole. They should withstand chewing and rough play and be discarded when they are worn out.
- Never – *even for a moment* – leave your dog loose and unattended with babies or young children no matter how well-mannered it is.

OUTDOORS

- Ensure that food put out for birds and wild animals cannot be reached by your dog. Pick up any dead birds or animals.
- Avoid growing mistletoe, yew trees and laburnum and a number of other plants that can be poisonous to your dog. Seek advice from a good garden centre.
- Take particular care if dogs have access to a garage or garden shed. Antifreeze, old paint, wood preservatives, glues, weed killers, fungicides and slug pellets are all of particular concern.
- Garages and sheds are best kept firmly shut and declared 'no go' areas.
- Use garden sprays very carefully and don't allow your dog access to sprayed

areas at least until the spray is dry.

- Remove drinking bowls before spraying with weed killer or dusting with ant powder or the like.
- Make sure that swimming pools and ponds are dog-safe.
- Keep your dog on the lead on busy roads no matter how obedient it is and put it on its lead before you get out of the car first with your dog following.
- Make sure all rubbish from the house or garden is securely wrapped and placed in a dustbin that can be properly closed.
- Check garden boundaries regularly.
- Travelling with a dog loose in a car is not illegal as long as the dog does not interfere with the driver. However, it is sensible to fit a dog guard, use a dog crate firmly fixed to the back seat or restrain your dog in a purpose-designed dog harness. A 50km/h (30mph) crash would throw a 20kg (50lb) dog forward with enough force to injure it severely and possibly kill the driver or a passenger. Small dogs can travel safely in the foot-well in front of the passenger at least for short distances but they do prefer to see where they are going!
- Do not let your dog put its head outside the car window.

DOG OWNER'S SURVIVAL KITS

As a dog owner it is sensible to keep a survival/first aid kit available in your house and in your car. The essential items to include are noted below and should be kept in an air-tight, strong metal tin that can be firmly closed. You may need the kit to help your own dog or another that it is trouble.

- Tweezers with rounded, not sharp pointed, ends.
- Curved-on-flat and straight blunt-ended scissors.
- Nail clippers (not the guillotine type).
- Strip of strong tape for use as an emergency muzzle.
- Two good crepe bandages (2-inch and 3-inch in width).
- A disinfectant – TCP or a specialized pet product from your veterinary surgeon.
- Liquid paraffin.
- Roll of 2-inch wide adhesive plaster.
- Rolls of 2-inch and 3-inch wide open weave cotton bandages.
- Large pad of cotton wool.
- A gauze pad.
- A pair of artery forceps (small scissor-action clamps that are obtainable from a chemist or veterinary surgery).
- A length of strong cotton-covered elastic for use as a tourniquet possibly with the use of artery forceps.
- A spare lead and collar.

Note: It is also sensible to keep in the car an old sheet or blanket which can be used to cover a sick or wounded dog to keep it warm. A plastic dustbin liner can also be of use if the ground is wet.

PREVENTING AND COPING

PART 3

CONTENTS

- **THE RELEVANCE OF THE SIGNS OF ILLNESS** Page 90
- **RECORD KEEPING AND HEALTH CHECKS** Page 91
- **WHAT TO TELL YOUR VET** Page 92
- **MAJOR INFECTIOUS DISEASES AND CONDITIONS** Page 93
- **PREVENTION OF ILLNESS** Page 146

WHAT IFs...?

What if my dog...
79 keeps breaking wind? Page 120
80 is biting its tail, scooting or rubbing its bottom on the ground? Page 121
81 has diarrhoea? Page 122
82 is passing blood in its faeces? Page 123
83 is constipated? Page 123

What if my dog...
84 is not passing urine or is straining to pass small amounts frequently? Page 124
85 & **106** is incontinent? Page 124, 141
86 is passing blood in its urine? Page 125
87 has a discharge from its penis or vulva (or licks excessively at its genitals)? Page 126
102 is over-sexed? Page 138
105 is passing urine more frequently? Page 140
107 is passing blood-stained, smelly urine with difficulty? Page 141
110 is licking her vulva excessively? Page 142
111 has a vaginal discharge? Page 143
112 is mated by accident? Page 143

What if my dog...
67 is in danger of becoming obese? Page 104
88 & **108** is pot-bellied? Page 126, 141
113 is found to be pregnant unexpectedly? Page 144
114 has signs of abdominal pain? Page 144

WITH ILLNESS

What if my dog...
74 is shaking or scratching its ears? Page 112
75 is holding its head on one side? Page 114
93 is having fits, convulsions or is twitching?
Page 132
100 appears deaf? Page 138

What if my dog...
71 has runny eyes? Page 109
72 has eyes that look
abnormal? Page 110
73 is blind? Page 112

What if my dog...
70 sneezes? Page 109
76 is breathing abnormally? Page 114
90 is coughing? Page 129
99 is not breathing? Page 137

What if my dog...
64 eats grass? Page 102
65 vomits? Page 102
66 refuses to eat? Page 104
68 is eating well but remains very thin? Page 108
69 & **103** is drinking excessively? Page 108, 140
91 is eating with difficulty? Page 130
92 has bad breath? Page 130
101 is salivating excessively? Page 138

What if my dog...
94 & **109** has a lump or swelling?
Page 133, 142
95 is wounded, grazed, cut, burnt or
scalded? Page 134
96 is licking itself excessively? Page 136
97 is weak and lethargic? Page 136
98 has collapsed and is
comatose? Page 136

What if my dog...
77 is shedding hair? Page 116
78 is scratching excessively? Page 117
89 is limping? Page 128
104 is going bald? Page 140
115 is a problem when on heat? Page 144

THE RELEVANCE OF THE SIGNS OF ILLNESS

Definitions

Signs of illness are objective evidence of an illness which can be recognized by an observant owner, for example coughing, diarrhoea, thirst etc. Symptoms are changes in bodily functions experienced by the sufferer, for example, pain or headache. Because dogs can't talk, they cannot tell anyone how they 'feel' and what they are experiencing. However, astute owners who know their pet well in normal health may be able to make an informed guess as to how the patient is feeling and in what way it is suffering.

The Interpretation of Signs of Illness

In the case of many common diseases the signs shown by affected dogs are all much the same, and furthermore not all affected dogs show all the signs characteristic of the disease in question. This means that attempting to make a diagnosis and identify the cause can be extremely difficult for owners in many instances. Very often it becomes necessary and sensible to seek the help of an experienced veterinary surgeon who may need to carry out laboratory tests and other procedures to confirm a tentative diagnosis. Left in isolation owners may well jump to the wrong conclusion and that could lead to delayed or ineffective treatment and more suffering for their pet.

Because of the difficulties noted above it was decided, when planning this book, that it would probably be of greater help to pet owners if information was given in respect of presenting signs, rather than describing the diseases themselves in the more conventional way. Hopefully this will allow owners to identify more readily when their pet is just off colour, or when it has a more serious disease or condition. In short the objective is to help owners identify and describe accurately the signs of illness and pain in their pet, to build up a meaningful 'history' of the problem, and to know if and when veterinary advice should be sought.

Recognizing The Early Signs of Illness

- **Changed behaviour** Any variation from a dog's normal behaviour that is not provoked by a notable change in circumstances may well indicate that a dog is generally unwell.
- **Refusal to eat (inappetence)** Refusal to eat is often the first sign of illness but is only of real significance if it persists for more than a few days.
- **Raised temperature** Dogs with raised temperatures will seek a cooler place to lie, they will pant and may feel hot to the

If any of the signs noted here persist for more than two to three days, consider seeking veterinary assistance.

touch. In general it is not advisable for owners to try to establish their dog's actual temperature, since any reading obtained needs a degree of interpretation.

- **General weakness and lethargy** If not associated with hot weather or excessive exercise, these signs could indicate some systemic disease. If the signs persist for more than two to three days, a veterinary investigation is warranted.
- **Pain** Pain is evidenced by crying (unprovoked vocalization), cringing and possibly aggression. Dogs in pain will usually turn and glance at the source of the pain and possibly bite at the affected area, they are often reluctant to leave their beds and generally resent the site of the pain being touched.

RECORD KEEPING AND HEALTH CHECKS

Keeping Records

Keeping a record of the major events relating to health in your dog's life is most important in respect of both the treatment and prevention of disease. Such a record will help you to provide a meaningful and complete history should you need to seek professional help. This could well lead to more prompt and effective treatment or preventive measures and save you time, expense and worry. It will also spare your dog from suffering unnecessarily.

Obtain a loose-leaf notebook and work out for yourself what to record and in what depth. You should, however, aim to include details under the following headings:

- Facts relating to your dog – its name, breed, sex, date of birth, a photograph and a description of any unique markings and scars etc.
  - Your veterinary surgeon's telephone number and other details relating to the practice, especially out-of-hours service.
    - Insurance details.
    - Record of vaccinations given.
    - Notes relating to any illnesses and the medication given.
      - For bitches a record of dates of being 'on heat' ('in season') and breeding history.
      - Your dog's weight every month for the first six months in your care and thereafter two or three times a year.

91

WHAT TO TELL YOUR VET

BE PREPARED TO TELL YOUR VET

- about your records and, if necessary, show them to him.
- when you first noticed the signs of illness, what you observed and in what order. Did the signs become progressively more severe or diminish in nature? Are they worse at any specific time of the day?

- if your pet is drinking more than usual. If so, give an indication of how much per day.
- if you have any other pets, are they too showing signs of illness?
- about your dog's appetite, is it eating or not? Is it having a problem picking up food, or swallowing it? Is it eating less than, or more than, usual? Have you made any changes to what your dog is fed?

- if your circumstances have changed. Have you introduced another animal, moved house, had decorators in, changed the carpets or your pet's bedding etc?
- if you have been on holiday with your dog. If so, was that in the UK or overseas?
- if your dog has been in contact with other dogs, e.g. in kennels, at a show or as a visitor. Were, or are, any of those contacts ill?
- about your dog's faeces – have these changed recently in colour or consistency? Does the dog strain to pass faeces? Does it 'go' more or less frequently than usual?
- about changes in your garden. Have you introduced new plants, used pesticides or any other garden sprays, top-dressed the lawn or flowerbeds with chemical preparations?
- about the frequency of urination. Does your pet pass urine more frequently than usual or have any difficulty in that respect? Does the urine contain any blood? Is your pet incontinent?
- if your pet has had an accident or a fight of any sort. What was involved, how did it happen and when?

Do make a note of all the facts that relate to the questions posed above and take it with you so that you can refer to your findings during the veterinary consultation. It's only too easy to forget important information during the anxiety and hassle of a visit to a veterinary surgery!

Usually the information referred to in the box on page 92 can only be supplied by an observant owner so you have a very important function to perform in contributing towards the restoration of your pet to good health. The history which you supply can be crucial in allowing the vet to make a correct diagnosis and help to ensure a rapid recovery.

MAJOR INFECTIOUS DISEASES AND CONDITIONS

Canine Diseases That Can Be Prevented By Vaccination – All Dogs

Six serious infectious diseases threaten dogs throughout their lives.
CANINE DISTEMPER – Cause: A viral infection readily spread by the inhalation of virus particles in droplets of moisture in the air.
Signs: Affected dogs initially have runny eyes, diarrhoea, a discharge from the nose and a severe cough. These signs are often followed by hardening of the foot pads and nervous signs, including fits, which frequently prove fatal.

INFECTIOUS CANINE HEPATITIS – Cause: A highly contagious viral disease which can be fatal within as little as 24 hours allowing no time for effective treatment.
Signs: The initial signs include loss of appetite, fever, pale or congested mucous membranes, vomiting, severe diarrhoea often containing blood, and acute abdominal pain. This infection can also cause liver and kidney damage in the long-term and may affect the eyes (Blue eye).

RABIES – Cause: A serious viral infection causing a change in temperament, fever, itching at the site of infection.
Signs: Hyperexcitability, extreme restlessness, salivation, depraved appetite, difficulty in swallowing, convulsions, paralysis, coma and death. Once signs are seen infected animals usually die within two weeks. The dumb (i.e. non-aggressive) form of rabies is unusual in dogs. This is a dangerous zoonosis – i.e. the disease affects both animals and people.

Preventive Measures

Fortunately effective vaccines are now available to protect dogs against all the infectious diseases noted here. Their use can give pet owners and dog breeders peace of mind, save dogs from suffering and prevent pets from dying prematurely. Veterinary advice is required so that the most cost-effective vaccination programme can be selected in any specific situation.

If you suspect that your dog is suffering from any of the diseases described above, and especially if it has not been vaccinated against them routinely, veterinary attention should be sought without delay.

Other Diseases and Conditions – All Dogs

CANINE PARVOVIRUS INFECTION – Cause: A very serious disease which can cause heart problems and pneumonia in young puppies.

Signs: In older puppies and adults severe vomiting and diarrhoea (often containing large amounts of blood). The disease may be rapidly fatal in very young puppies and also in older dogs if treatment is delayed.

LEPTOSPIROSIS – Cause: The two forms of leptospirosis are caused by bacteria called leptospires.

Signs: Affected dogs run a high temperature, vomit severely and often become jaundiced. Those dogs which do not die may suffer from chronic liver or kidney damage later in life. These infections can be passed on to people.

KENNEL COUGH – Cause: An irritating disease complex which can be caused by a number of infectious agents including the bacterium *Bordetella bronchiseptica* and a number of viruses, particularly canine parainfluenza, canine herpes and canine adeno viruses, acting alone or in combination, and possible exacerbated by secondary bacterial infection.

Signs: The signs consist of a harsh dry cough which can persist for as long as three weeks. Affected dogs do not usually have a raised temperature and they continue to eat quite normally. Severe coughing episodes can end up with gagging and retching so that owners frequently think that an infected dog may have a bone stuck in its throat.

Apart from the diseases mentioned above it has recently become possible to vaccinate dogs against canine herpesvirus infection and canine coronovirus infection. The former virus, as well as having a role in kennel cough, is one of the causes of death in young puppies and the latter virus is now considered as being responsible for a higher frequency of canine enteritis than previously realized.

Some other major diseases and conditions affecting all dogs also call for veterinary assistance since diagnosis of the cause is required so that effective treatment can be instigated. They are described briefly below.

ALLERGY – Cause: Hypersensitivity to various allergens which may be inhaled (e.g. house dust mites and pollen), ingested (e.g. an allergy to a variety of foods), or through direct contact (e.g. with

Insect stings can sometimes cause an allergic reaction. Treatment with antihistamines and/or corticosteroids may be required.

dyes in carpets and furnishings). An allergic response may also occur as a result of insect bites or stings.

Signs: Usually inflammation of the skin causing itching (pruritus), scratching, hair loss and open sores which may then become infected by bacteria. Allergic reactions are only very occasionally manifested in dogs as an asthma attack, anaphylaxis (extreme sensitivity to a particular allergen), or chronic diarrhoea.

Action: *Seek veterinary help without delay.* Most cases respond quickly to the administration of antihistamines or corticosteroids applied topically or given by injection or by mouth. Prevention involves avoiding contact with known allergens.

CONGESTIVE HEART FAILURE – Cause: Subsequent to left- or right-sided heart failure which may be congenital, or acquired, as a result of lesions affecting the heart valves or the blood and nerve supply to the heart muscles.

Signs: Breathlessness, coughing – especially at night, lethargy, weakness, poor appetite, weight loss.

Action: A prompt veterinary consultation is needed since treatment involves the administration of diuretics, cardiac and respiratory stimulants and products to control the heart rate. Vitamin F supplementation can be beneficial in some cases. Prevention relies on weight reduction, the avoidance of stressful conditions and regular controlled exercise. Importantly salt levels in the diet should be kept low.

DIABETES MELLITUS – Cause: Lack of insulin production by the pancreas or failure of the tissues to respond to the effect of the hormone leading to raised blood sugar levels.

Signs: Excessive thirst, increased frequency of urination, a voracious appetite, weight loss, vomiting, laboured breathing, depression and dehydration. Rapidly developing cataracts may also be noticed.

Action: Veterinary advice should be sought promptly to confirm the diagnosis and the severity of the condition. The administration of insulin and dietary control – usually involving a high fibre diet – needs to be under veterinary supervision. Feeding a consistent diet at regular intervals is important. In the case of bitches, spaying can be helpful.

EPILEPSY – Cause: Abnormal electrical discharges of unknown origin in the brain. A predisposition to the condition may be inherited or associated with age and sex.

Loss of consciousness may occur as a result of an attack of epilepsy, which is also characterized by fits.

Signs: Fits and convulsions occurring when the dog is relaxed or sleeping followed by collapse and loss of consciousness, confusion, depression, loss of balance, an increased desire to eat and/or drink, and possibly blindness.
Action: Seek veterinary help. Continual medication through the dog's life is usually required.

SHOCK – Cause: Collapse of the circulatory system resulting from haemorrhage, trauma, burns, anaphylaxis (extreme sensitivity to an allergen), an accumulation of toxins in the blood, or cardiac failure.
Signs: Collapse, muscle weakness, subnormal body temperature and cold extremities, coma, rapid feeble pulse, and dilated pupils.
Action: *Seek veterinary attention urgently.* Treatment usually involves the administration of fluids, by intravenous infusion, corticosteroids and possibly cardiac stimulants.

BLADDER STONES – Cause: Stones (calculae) in the urinary tract are usually caused by a bacterial infection of the bladder or possibly liver disease resulting in a change of urine pH, hormone imbalance, inadequate fluid intake, or possibly a vitamin A deficiency.
Signs: Frequent straining to pass urine which is often bloodstained, depression and loss of appetite.
Action: Seek veterinary attention since the appropriate treatment depends largely on the composition of the stones. Generally the administration of antibiotics and urinary disinfectants is required. Prevention relies principally of the control of urine pH, and usually adjustments to the dog's diet are required.

Some breeds, especially Dalmatians, are more susceptible to bladder stones than others.

Male Dogs

PROSTATIC HYPERPLASIA – Cause: An increase in the size of the prostate gland probably as a result of changing hormonal balance with age. If there is excessive growth, it can affect the rectum (the urethra is unlikely to be affected as happens in men).
Signs: Constipation with the production of ribbon-like faeces and straining which may cause a perineal hernia. Bleeding from the penis or prepuce may be seen and there is sometimes blood in the urine.
Action: Castration or the administration of sex hormones usually brings about a cure. Surgical removal of the prostate gland in dogs is difficult and the results are frequently disappointing.

TESTICULAR PROBLEMS

CRYPTORCHIDISM is the failure of one or both of the testicles to descend into the scrotum by six months of age. This condition is

inherited in most cases. Retention of both testes usually results in sterility. Because there is a much higher frequency of tumours in retained testicles, surgical removal is usually recommended.

TESTICULAR NEOPLASIA These tumours are sometimes malignant but more often benign. In some cases affected dogs may become attractive to other dogs. Depending on the type of tumour, affected testicles may or may not be enlarged.

ORCHITIS (Inflammation of the testes) – Cause: May be caused by trauma but usually as a result of a bacterial infection.
Signs: In acute cases hot, swollen, painful testicles. In the chronic state affected testicles are firmer and often nodular in shape. Dogs with orchitis often have a stiff gait.
Action: *Seek veterinary help without delay* since a course of antibiotics is generally required.

Bitches

A number of major diseases and conditions are specific to bitches. Some details relating to those of special significance are noted below. See also Feminine Problems on pages 140-145.

ECLAMPSIA (Lactation tetany) – Cause: This condition is caused by lowered levels of calcium and possibly glucose in the blood.
Signs: Signs occur in bitches which have whelped up to 21 days previously. Characteristically, affected bitches become anxious, restless, hide from light, reject their puppies, salivate, become incoordinate, have muscle spasms and convulsions followed, in the absence of treatment, by coma and death.
Action: *This is a true veterinary emergency – seek veterinary attention without delay.* Intravenous injections of calcium and glucose usually bring about a very rapid recovery. No specific action can be taken to prevent the condition, but it is important *not* to oversupplement with calcium during pregnancy.

Bitches that are suffering from false pregnancy may become nervous and start to carry toys, shoes and other objects around the house.

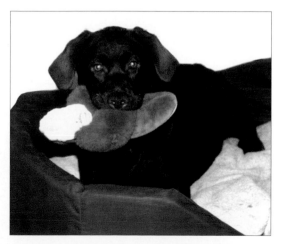

FALSE PREGNANCY – Cause: The cause is obscure but possibly results from an hormonal imbalance.
Signs: Characteristically affected bitches

97

show the signs of pregnancy, nursing and milk production and yet produce no puppies either because they have not been mated or have failed to conceive. They often have a distended abdomen and an increased appetite.

The signs occur one to two months after the bitch has been on heat and vary greatly in type and severity. Most bitches, however, will produce some milk and display maternal behaviour. Many will have nervous signs including restlessness and carrying shoes and toys around the house and taking them to their beds. A bitch that has suffered from the condition once is likely to experience it again after each subsequent heat with the signs becoming progressively more severe and protracted.

Action: If the signs are mild, it is probably better not to give any medication or treatment. The nervous signs will disappear more quickly if the bitch is denied sympathy and if toys and brooding objects are removed. Less milk will be produced if exercise levels are increased and the carbohydrate content of the diet reduced.

If the signs are severe and the above actions do not help, veterinary advice should be sought. Hormone tablets or injections may help to relieve the more specific signs and sedatives may be required to control the nervous signs.

Prevention: Owners are often advised to have their bitch spayed if it has severe false pregnancies, since bitches that do not come on heat do not suffer from false pregnancy. The chemical control of heat may advocated by vets in some instances.

PYOMETRA – Cause: In this condition large amounts of fluid accumulate in the uterus, characteristically one to two months after a bitch has been on heat. The cause is not entirely clear, but is probably brought about by an hormonal imbalance.

Signs: Typically bitches with pyometra are obviously ill and depressed; they drink large amounts of water and urinate more frequently. The abdomen is often distended and the bitch may have a raised temperature. In so-called 'open' cases there is a thick reddish-brown evil smelling discharge from the vulva; there is no discharge in 'closed' cases. The condition is most often seen in older bitches, six to seven years of age, that have not had puppies. The signs can be variable, so diagnosis is not always easy.

Action: If an owner suspects that their bitch is suffering from this condition, *it is essential that veterinary advice is sought without delay* since an emergency operation to remove the uterus and ovaries is usually needed to save the bitch. Some open cases may respond to medical treatment and this course of action may be advisable for cases in which anaesthesia and major surgery may be considered more risky.

MAMMARY TUMOURS – Cause: Unknown but may be sex hormone dependent; there is possibly an inherited disposition. **Signs:** Swellings/lumps in the mammary glands – one or more glands may be affected. As many as 75 per cent of bitches develop mammary tumours (growths in the mammary glands) as they get older. It makes sense to inspect the mammary glands of bitches regularly so that any swellings can be identified early. **Action:** If lumps are felt, their size should be recorded and monitored carefully under veterinary supervision and advice taken on their possible removal before the tumour has a chance to spread to other organs in the body; a situation which occurs all to often. Fortunately, many such growths are not malignant and are relatively easily removed surgically, provided they have not been allowed to grow too large. There is some evidence that the chemical control of heat may reduce the incidence of mammary tumours and spaying early in life has a similar effect.

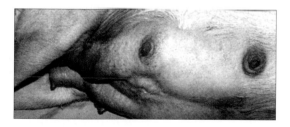

Mastitis is inflammation of the mammary glands; a course of antibiotic medication is usually required to effect a cure.

MASTITIS – Cause: Inflammation of the mammary glands usually caused by a bacterial infection in lactating bitches. Mastitis may occur in breeding bitches after whelping or during false pregnancy. **Signs:** Painful, hard, hot, swollen mammary glands and often the production of abnormal-looking or blood-stained milk. Very frequently only one gland is affected. The signs are accompanied by depression, fever, loss of appetite and vomiting. In some cases an abscess forms in the gland and this may burst to the outside. **Action:** Seek prompt veterinary assistance since administration of antibiotics by injection or by mouth is generally required. In some cases the administration of non-steroidal anti-inflammatory drugs (NSAIDs) may be helpful. Bathing the gland with warm salt water may help relieve the pain. In severe cases surgical drainage or excision of the affected gland may be necessary.

Internal Parasite Infections

Endoparasites are parasites which live inside the body as opposed to on its surface. A large number of worms can infest dogs but two are particularly common, namely the roundworm *Toxocara canis* and the tapeworm *Dipylidium caninum*.

ROUNDWORM INFECTION

- *Toxocara canis* is a white worm, 7.5-15cm (3-6in) in length.
- Currently, virtually all puppies born to bitches that have not been wormed during pregnancy will have adult worms in their intestines. They will be capable of laying eggs by the time the puppy is 21 to 30 days old.
- Puppies under three months old can be infected by eating worm eggs found on grass, plants in the garden, or on the bitch's coat. These hatch in the puppy's stomach, moving through the body and back to the intestine, where they become adult. Very young puppies can also be infected by immature worms in their mother's milk.
- In puppies more than three months of age, the larvae make only a limited migration and lie dormant in the body tissues, particularly in the muscles, the diaphragm and kidneys.
- When bitches become pregnant, the larvae lying dormant are stimulated to migrate again. They reach the womb and the mammary glands, infecting the puppies and completing the cycle.
- Around 30 to 40 per cent of puppies less than three months of age have adult worms in their intestines, which are able to pass eggs into the environment.
- Eggs in fresh faeces take 2-3 weeks to become infective to dogs or people.

TAPEWORM INFECTION

- This worm, which lives in the small intestines of dogs, is a flat, segmented worm that can measure up to 50cm (20in) in length.
- Fleas are a necessary part of the life cycle of *D. caninum*.
- Prevention of infection with this tapeworm requires a regular campaign against fleas on the dog and around the home.

Signs: Sometimes, in heavy roundworm infections, live worms are vomited. Tapeworm segments may be seen around the anus in infected dogs. However diagnosis is often difficult, as neither of these worms cause specific signs. Tapeworms rarely cause noticeable clinical signs apart from anal irritation and digestive disturbances, but roundworm infections may be associated with poor growth, diarrhoea, or constipation, abdominal pain, possibly a pot-bellied appearance and a decreased or increased appetite. Of course, all these signs can also be associated with other diseases.

Treatment: Worm tablets can be bought from either a chemist or from a pet shop, but it is necessary to know the type of worm infecting a dog in order to obtain the correct remedy.

It makes sense to speak to your vet if you are concerned. He or she may need to examine a sample of your dog's faeces to find out what eggs are present so that the correct treatment can be prescribed. In the case of *D. caninum* infection, your vet will also advise you how to control fleas.

These examples of the roundworm Toxocara canis *were recovered from one dog.*

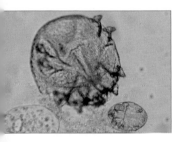

The ectoparasite Sarcoptes *illustrated here is a cause of mange in dogs.*

Worming dogs is a complicated matter and new products are continually being developed. It is important, therefore, to be guided by your veterinary surgeon and obtain advice in respect of regular worming regimes.

ADVICE ON ELIMINATING ROUNDWORM

The elimination of the roundworm *Toxocara canis* is important because it can cause problems in people. Such cases are highlighted from time to time in the media and are often exaggerated by the anti-dog lobby. If everyone who owns a dog follows the simple advice given below, the already low risk of damage to sight, which may be associated with this infection in children, could be reduced still further and possibly even eliminated.

Puppies

- Puppies should be wormed regularly from 2-5 weeks of age as directed by a veterinary surgeon.
- Puppies should be trained to defecate in a specific fenced-off area in the garden before they are taken for walks.
- Faeces from dogs less than six months old must be picked up promptly and be buried deeply or flushed down the toilet.
- Dogs under six months of age should not be exercised in public places where children play or where families picnic.

Adult dogs

- For routine control of roundworms and tapeworms, treatment at three-monthly intervals is usually recommended.

Adult bitches

- All entire bitches should be wormed during pregnancy with a product that is effective against migrating larvae. The usual regime adopted is daily medication from day 40 of pregnancy through to two days post whelping.
- If you own a bitch, speak to your vet about controlling heat in your pet. Bitches that do not come on heat are, like dogs, much less likely to pass on infection. In entire bitches, worming during false pregnancy has been recommended.

EXTERNAL PARASITE INFECTIONS

Parasites that live on or in the skin are called ectoparasites. The ectoparasites that most commonly infect dogs in the UK are fleas, lice, ticks, harvest mites, and mange mites.

Collectively these are probably the major cause of skin disease in dogs. Unfortunately the signs of skin disease are not generally specific for any one infection, thus diagnosis of the cause, often involving laboratory tests, is necessary if the most appropriate treatment is to be given.

Details relating particularly to fleas and lice are given under the heading 'What if my dog is scratching excessively?' (See 'What if?' no.78).

What if my dog eats grass?

64 Many dogs eat small amounts of coarse grass quite regularly, only for it to be vomited, covered in frothy saliva, a few minutes later. If this habit causes inconvenience, it may help to give two or three small meals a day rather than one large meal.

If grass eating is accompanied by prolonged or persistent vomiting, and particularly if the vomit contains blood, *veterinary advice should be sought quickly*.

What if my dog vomits?

65 Vomiting is part of the body's defence mechanism, enabling the stomach to get rid of any excess food, water or unsuitable or decayed matter before it passes further into the digestive system and causes harm.

Dogs vomit easily, and occasional incidents are to be expected and are unimportant. On the other hand, prolonged or persistent true vomiting, particularly if the vomit contains blood, requires *immediate veterinary attention*. Two types of vomiting are recognized: true vomiting and regurgitation.

TRUE VOMITING

Significance: This involves movement of the muscles of the abdomen, chest or diaphragm (i.e. heaving) in order to eject the contents of the stomach. The main danger of repeated or continuous true vomiting is dehydration (loss of body fluids), which can be recognized by picking up a fold of skin on the dog's back between your thumb and forefinger. If the fold remains 'tented' when you release it, that indicates the dog is dehydrated, and *prompt action is called for*. Fluid replacement, possibly small quantities given frequently by mouth, but more often by means of an intravenous drip may be required. Steroids may need to be administered to overcome shock and specific antiemetic compounds may be required to prevent further vomiting.

Cause: True vomiting may be caused by a great variety of diseases, conditions and factors. Not surprisingly therefore veterinary surgeons frequently have to rely on laboratory tests and other diagnostic investigations, such as radiography, in order to make a meaningful diagnosis so that the most appropriate and effective treatment can be given. As noted above vomiting may be associated with:

Dogs that scavenge food may eat rotting carrion or some other unsuitable material that will cause them to vomit.

- **Serious diseases and conditions** in the dog, particularly canine parvovirus disease, kidney disease, and pyometra in bitches. In these diseases vomiting will usually be accompanied by loss of appetite, raised body temperature, depression and diarrhoea. *Veterinary help is needed at once particularly if the vomit contains blood.*
- **Eating unsuitable or decayed material,** carrion or plant material which has been sprayed with toxic substances; or bad food. In such cases the signs mentioned above may be accompanied by drooling from the mouth and signs of abdominal pain. *Veterinary help is needed urgently.*
- **Intestinal obstructions** are a relatively frequent cause of vomiting in dogs, particularly puppies. Vomiting may result from stones, toys, bones and stolen objects becoming lodged in the digestive tract. Twists in the bowel, or the telescoping of one part of the bowel into another (intussusception), are relatively common causes of vomiting in young puppies. If you suspect that your dog has swallowed a toy, ball or a bone, *it is important to consult a vet at once* as surgery may be required.
- **Travel sickness** – see Part 1, 'What if?' no.12.
- **Bloating** – see 'What if?' no.88.

Treatment: Very effective antiemetics are available to veterinary surgeons these days. They must be used with caution because they may mask an important underlying cause. It is most important for owners to follow the instructions given in respect of dosage.

Importantly medicines designed to prevent or treat travel sickness in people should not be given to dogs. It is also wrong to allow a vomiting dog to drink its fill of cold water. Instead, very small amounts should be offered every half an hour or so.

Once your dog shows signs of wanting to start eating again, begin by giving small meals of easily digested food such as scrambled egg or boiled fish and then gradually return to normal diet. Special diets for convalescing dogs are also available.

If the dog is known to have eaten a poisonous substance, e.g. a garden chemical or slug bait, take the original container with you to the veterinary surgeon, as the manufacturer's analysis may be helpful in tracing an antidote to the poison.

REGURGITATION

Regurgitation is a more passive action used to bring up boluses of recently eaten food. When freshly eaten food is regurgitated the dog may eat it again at once, and this behaviour is normal in some dogs, particularly when they bolt their food in competition with other dogs. Persistent regurgitation in an older puppy especially, or an adult dog, may indicate some obstruction or malformation in the gullet and *this condition warrants prompt veterinary advice*.

103

What if my dog refuses to eat?

66 While loss of appetite may be the first sign of a major illness and needs to be monitored closely, it is also not uncommon for a healthy, well-fed dog to refuse a meal occasionally, often for the reasons listed below.

- Puppies may temporarily refuse to eat newly introduced foods.
- Refusal of food is normal and sensible when a dog is exhausted by vigorous exercise.
- Dogs will often refuse food when they have other things on their minds, for instance a bitch in season nearby.
- Food refusal may be due to environmental stress; guard dogs will not eat when strangers are present and pet dogs in boarding kennels may starve themselves for a few days.
- Most bitches will refuse food for a day or part of a day during pregnancy.

Persistent refusal of food, especially if accompanied by other signs of illness, needs careful monitoring. Veterinary help should be sought if all food is refused for more that 24 hours in a young puppy or 48 hours in an adult, provided none of the situations mentioned above are pertinent.

What if my dog is in danger of becoming obese?

67 It is normal for many dogs to 'gorge feed' if they have the opportunity This habit is often intensified when there are other animals in the household.

Most veterinary surgeons recommend that dogs are fed commercially produced complete diets either canned, dry or moist. If your dog is fed in that way it is important to follow the manufacturer's instructions regarding the amount fed and the frequency of feeding. Such a diet can be supplemented with human leftovers such as the remains of a stew, uneaten cooked eggs or fish (be wary of bones!). However, such food should not make up more than 10 per cent of the dog's standard diet otherwise the balance of essential nutrients could be upset. The amount of food your dog is given must always be in *your* control, don't give your dog the chance to eat more than it should. Should your dog be eating really frantically and starting to eat normally inedible things, seek veterinary help since it may be suffering from a specific

Diseases and conditions associated with obesity

- Arthritis and other orthopaedic conditions
- Diabetes mellitus
- Heat intolerance
- Heart failure
- Impaired digestion (flatulence)
- Increased susceptibility to disease
- Reduced liver function
- Reproductive problems
- Skin disease
- Reduced life expectancy

Tips for Successful Slimming

- Establish a goal.
- Decide on a dietary regime.
- Weigh your dog regularly and monitor its girth.
- Aim for a gradual weight loss.
- Increase the amount of exercise your dog gets.
- Feed your dog small meals more frequently than usual from a smaller bowl.
- Convince everyone (in the family and any visitors) how important it is for your dog to lose weight.

disease or condition, such as diabetes, or possibly a parasite infection.

Obesity is the single most common nutritional problem faced by dogs and people in the developed world. Current estimates indicate that more than one dog in three is overweight. The cause of obesity is quite simply eating more food than is required by the body, the result being that the excess calories are stored as fat in a number of different places and organs. Unfortunately obesity develops gradually so pet owners often do not notice from day to day any change in the health, weight and size of their dog and only recognize the problem when the dog is grossly overweight. Obesity is only very rarely caused by hormonal problems.

A considerable number of diseases and conditions have been linked with obesity. The list (table left) emphasizes clearly the need to slim an obese dog rather than allow it to struggle on in discomfort, and possibly pain, to an early death.

Treatment: Although it is possible for pet owners to devise a diet that is low in calories, particularly those derived from fat, to bring about weight loss, or simply to reduce the amount of food given, this is not easy and is difficult to implement. There is the real danger too that the dog will resort to begging and scavenging and that someone in the family will

Don't over-indulge a favourite pet – obesity is a serious health risk.

capitulate. Furthermore there is a risk that the dog may become deficient in some essential nutrient. In short it makes sense to consult your vet – you may well find that the practice runs special clinics for overweight dogs. You will not only be able to obtain good advice and the all important follow-up on results but also purchase special 'light' diets that are produced by a number of major dog food companies. Whatever special advice you receive, it is important that you follow the principles noted (table left) to help ensure success and so that your dog will lose the right amount of weight reasonably quickly and permanently.

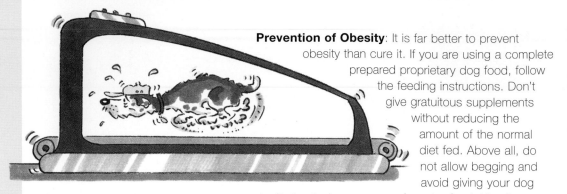

Prevention of Obesity: It is far better to prevent obesity than cure it. If you are using a complete prepared proprietary dog food, follow the feeding instructions. Don't give gratuitous supplements without reducing the amount of the normal diet fed. Above all, do not allow begging and avoid giving your dog any opportunity to steal or scavenge for extra food. Use the fitness assessment score card to check your dog's condition and if you have any doubts seek help from your veterinary surgery.

Regular exercise is important to combat obesity.

IS YOUR DOG FIT OR FAT? – FITNESS ASSESSMENT SCORE CARD

The questions have been designed so that your final score will give an indication of the fitness of your dog. Answer them truthfully, don't make excuses and be prepared to take the appropriate actions suggested.

1 Which shape does your dog most closely resemble? 1, 2 or 3?

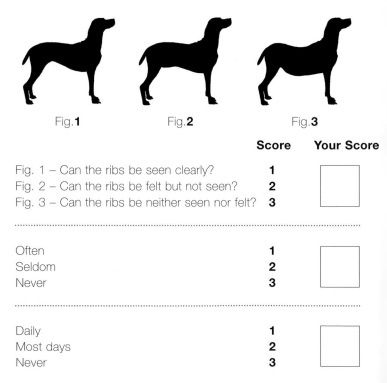

Fig.**1**   Fig.**2**   Fig.**3**

	Score	Your Score
Fig. 1 – Can the ribs be seen clearly?	1	
Fig. 2 – Can the ribs be felt but not seen?	2	
Fig. 3 – Can the ribs be neither seen nor felt?	3	

2 Does your dog exercise itself by playing with a ball?		
Often	1	
Seldom	2	
Never	3	

3 Do you take your dog for a good walk?		
Daily	1	
Most days	2	
Never	3	

		Score	Your Score
4 Is your dog keen to go for a walk regardless of the weather?	Always Sometimes Never	1 2 3	
5 After moderate exercise, such as a run around the garden, does your dog pant?	Never Sometimes Always	1 2 3	
6 Does your dog pant when lying in the sun outside and move to a cooler place?	Never Sometimes Often	1 2 3	
7 Does your dog beg for scraps?	Never Sometimes Often	1 2 3	
8 Does your dog refuse some foods?	Never Sometimes Often	1 2 3	
9 Does your dog eat its meal completely within five minutes?	Never Sometimes Often	1 2 3	

Add **2** to your score if you don't know – or are unsure about – the answer to any question.

Your total score:

	Score	Action
The score can only act as a guide. If you are in doubt, consult your veterinary surgeon.	**10-14**	Normal fit dog.
	15-20	Dog tending to be fat. Start dietary control and increase exercise.
	21-24	Overweight, seek veterinary advice.
	25-30	Greatly overweight, seek veterinary advice *urgently*.

What if my dog is eating well but remains very thin?

68 This can be a normal situation in adolescent dogs of the larger breeds, especially where more than one dog is kept and there is continual activity. If your dog is just thinner than you would like, first check that you are feeding it correctly and make any necessary adjustments. Serious emaciation may be caused by many infectious diseases, dietary deficiency or imbalance, endoparasite infection, cancer, liver or kidney disease, mouth problems, intestinal problems, diabetes and some hormonal deficiencies. Obviously if your dog is giving real cause for concern, seek veterinary help since it is essential to diagnose the cause of the problem and instigate the most appropriate medication and any other procedures that are necessary. It is a waste of time and money to purchase medicine or special energy-dense diets that may not be necessary and which are not specific for the particular problem.

What if my dog is drinking excessively?

69 It is always useful for owners to have a note of the quantity of water that their dog drinks normally. Some common causes of dogs drinking more than usual (polydipsia) include:

Strenuous exercise on a hot day will naturally make a dog thirsty. However, it may be a sign of illness if your dog continues to drink a lot at home.

- Abnormally hot weather.
- Excessive exercise.
- Eating food containing extra salt or drinking sea water.
- Lactation – bitches with litters need to drink a lot of water to ensure full milk production.

None of these is of particular concern but excessive drinking in other circumstances is a significant sign of illness and could be associated with diabetes mellitus or diabetes insipidus, chronic kidney failure, adrenal or thyroid malfunctions, liver disease, toxaemia (the spread of toxins in the blood), pyometra in bitches (see page 98), or mental problems. It is occasionally caused by medication, e.g. corticosteroid therapy. All these conditions are potentially serious and so veterinary consultation should not be delayed.

What if my dog sneezes?

70 It is normal for some dogs to sneeze two or three times when they wake up. An occasional bout of sneezing in dusty conditions, when being exercised on very dry ground, or when aerosol sprays or powders are being used is also normal.

A rapid fit of sneezing, accompanied by distress, shaking the head, rubbing the nose, with discharge or bleeding from the nostrils and noisy breathing may mean that a foreign body (a grass seed, twig or some other similar object) is lodged in the nose. Do not attempt any first aid but take the dog to the veterinary surgery *at once* since a proper diagnosis and complete removal of any foreign object is essential.

Sneezing, possibly with the addition of bleeding from the nostrils and perhaps with swelling and cuts on the face, may be caused by a blow to the nose, for example when the dog has run at speed into a hard object or been involved in a road traffic accident. Veterinary help will be needed to assess the extent of the injury.

Finally, bear in mind that sneezing may be a prelude to respiratory disease. If that is suspected, observe your dog closely for other signs that will indicate the need to seek veterinary help.

A blow on the nose can lead to bouts of sneezing.

What if my dog has runny eyes?

71 A slight, clear discharge from the eyes is normal in many dogs and in some breeds the shape of the face and eyelids in particular make a slight overspill of tears and subsequent staining of the hair around the eye, especially in white coated dogs, inevitable. The discharge should be carefully removed with damp cotton wool swab once a day or as often as necessary.

Where there is a pronounced staining on the face which threatens to become sore or ulcerated, veterinary advice should be sought as it is possible that surgical correction to the drainage from the eye can be made. An unaccustomed smoky atmosphere, or driving with the dog's head out of the car window may irritate the eyes and cause an excessive discharge. The latter habit is dangerous and should never be permitted.

If the discharge from the eyes is profuse, contains pus or is ▶

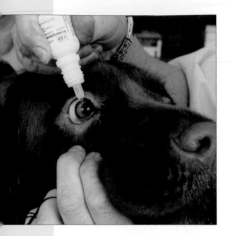

If your dog has eye problems, always seek expert advice from a vet. Sight is too important a sense to risk by delay or experimenting with over-the-counter medication.

accompanied by persistent signs of pain, ***veterinary advice should be sought without delay*** as any injury to the eyes can potentially lead to loss of sight, sometimes permanently.

Persistent discharge from the eyes, associated with conjunctivitis (inflammation of the inside lining of the eyelids, often with a pus-like discharge and crusting of the lids) may indicate that the dog is suffering from a major disease which requires prompt veterinary help.

Certain anatomical defects of the face and eye (either inherited or acquired), such as in-turning eyelashes (entropion) or an extra row of lashes (distichiasis), facial hair causing irritation to the surface of the eye or small or blocked drainage canals can also cause chronic conjunctivitis. Some surgical correction may be possible, but the veterinary surgeon is likely to advise that the dog or bitch should not be used for breeding or showing subsequently.

A dog's eyes are too important to risk delay or incorrect treatment, so ***veterinary consultation is always necessary*** and nothing but veterinary prescribed preparations should be used. Do not be tempted to use eye drops which have been prescribed for a previous condition or for human use.

What if my dog has eyes that look abnormal?

72

It makes sense to check regularly that your dog's eyes look normal. This examination is probably best done while you are grooming your dog. The sort of changes you may see and their significance are noted in the table opposite.

The blueish haze in this dog's eye is caused by glaucoma.

Some common inherited eye defects in dogs are:
- Progressive retinal atrophy (PRA) – progressive destruction of light-sensitive tissue at the back of the eye.
- Hereditary cataract – loss of transparency of the lens of the eye.
- Collie eye anomaly (CEA) – an eye defect very widespread in Collie breeds.
- Lens luxation – weakening or rupture of the ligaments holding the lens in place so that the lens falls forward into the front chamber of the eye.

If an inherited defect is suspected, your vet will usually arrange for your dog to be examined by an eye specialist. This is particularly important if you intend to breed from your pet.

Change noted	Possible cause	Recommended action
Bulging eyeball with the cornea looking a greeny-blue colour.	Glaucoma – caused by impaired drainage within the eye itself.	Consult a veterinary surgeon without delay.
Swollen eye lids.	Insect bites or stings or an allergic reaction.	Veterinary attention will usually alleviate the condition quickly.
Inability to raise upper eyelid (ptosis).	Malfunctioning facial nerves or sometimes general illness.	Consult a vet immediately.
An opaque patch on the surface of the eye (the cornea). Usually only one eye is affected.	Keratitis or a corneal ulcer. Associated with trauma to the eye, failure of tear production, or an hormonal deficiency.	Consult your vet without any delay. Prompt diagnosis of the cause and specific medication is essential
Blue eye. The whole cornea becomes opaque pale blue. Only one eye may be affected.	An aftermath of infectious canine hepatitis virus infection.	Recovery usually occurs in 3-4 weeks. Often the dog will be under a vet's care already for the systemic signs of the disease.
An opaqueness within the eye.	Cataract – an opacity of the lens in the eye which usually develops quite slowly, affecting vision to a varying degree. May be inherited.	Seek veterinary opinion if the blindness affects the dog's behaviour or quality of life. Surgical removal of the affected lens may be advocated
Protrusion of the third eyelid over the surface of the eye.	Usually loss of fat behind the eye through illness, poor condition or bad diet.	If the condition does not improve within a few days, seek veterinary attention
A red lump protruding at the inner corner of the eye.	Enlarged Harderian gland, known as 'cherry eye'. The cause is unclear.	Consult a veterinary surgeon without delay
Dilated pupils in good light	Several serious eye conditions including progressive retinal atrophy.	Prompt veterinary attention is essential.

What if my dog is blind?

73 Many elderly dogs become partially or completely blind, usually as a result of developing cataracts, but by using scent and hearing they can manage very well on familiar territory provided they are given a certain amount of consideration and unexpected hazards are not left in their path.

Loss of sight should not be a reason for having a well-loved older dog destroyed when it is otherwise healthy and its quality of life is not adversely affected.

Sudden blindness is a young or middle-aged dog needs *immediate* veterinary help. In a younger dog, veterinary advice should be obtained promptly as treatment may be possible, but only if the condition is recognized early. See also 'What if?' no.72.

What if my dog is shaking or scratching its ears?

74 It is important to be familiar with the appearance of your dog's normal, clean ears so that when you make your routine weekly inspection, you will be aware of any changes taking place. A small amount of light-brown waxy secretion is normal and necessary to the health of the ear, but there should be no unpleasant smell.

Many dogs shake their ears quite violently when arousing from sleep, and many also occasionally scratch their ears, but repeated violent head-shaking and/or scratching is a sign that something is wrong.

Signs: The following signs are indicative of an ear problem, particularly ear canker (otitis externa).

- Repeated scratching and head shaking.
- Head held with painful side downwards.
- Dark reddish-brown waxy deposits in the ear.
- An unpleasant smell from the ear.
- Inflammation – heat, swelling and pain in the canal and flap.

Causes: Otitis externa may be caused by a variety of factors including:

- Ear mites; small mange mites living in the ear.
- A fungus or yeast infection.
- Foreign bodies, e.g. grass awns or seeds.
- Allergy or an extension of skin disease.
- A variety of bacterial infections.

Keep an eye open for prolonged bouts of ear shaking and scratching – it may indicate that a problem exists in the ear canal.

Be gentle when plucking out excess hair growth from inside the ears. Your dog may find it uncomfortable.

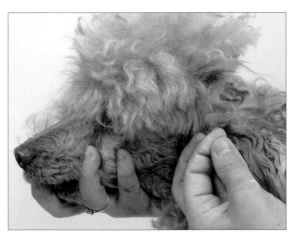

It is important to keep the inside surfaces of the ears clean but don't start probing inside the ear canal with cotton buds or pointed instruments. Just concentrate on the accessible surface areas.

- Poor ear conformation leading to inadequate ventilation of the ear canal, possibly associated with large floppy ears, or excessively hairy ear canals which can cause the retention of wax and debris leading to bacterial infection and inflammation.

Treatment: Any disease of the ears must be properly diagnosed and treated without delay, as a simple condition may progress rapidly into a more complex situation which can become difficult and expensive to treat, and which may create a smell which pervades the whole house. In addition, the acute pain caused by ear disease may make the dog irritable and inclined to snap when the ears are touched.

No attempt should be made to treat ear disease with proprietary remedies which may be inappropriate or useless for the particular condition affecting your dog. Always seek veterinary advice early as delay could mean that an operation will be required to cure the condition if it has become chronic. Early treatment can save you time and money and prevent your dog suffering.

Prevention:
- Keep the hair under the ear flaps combed free of burrs and tangles.
- Dry the dog's ears after bathing.
- Remove excess hair from the inside the ears by plucking or clipping, but be gentle. Failure to keep the vertical ear canal clear, clean and properly ventilated is often the root cause of otitis externa.
- Do not attempt to clean deeply inside the ear. Wipe the surface only with cotton wool, dampened with a weak disinfectant solution. Use only your fingers, never any kind of instrument or probe.

What if my dog is holding its head on one side?

The crusty, reddened areas on the sides of the ear canal are signs of otitis externa (ear canker).

75

This sign is usually indicative of an ear problem, see 'What if?' no.74, but may also be caused by teething around the age of 4-6 months in a puppy, or toothache in an older dog (see 'What if?' no.92) or by tonsillitis (see 'What if?' no.90).

Other possible causes of this sign include:

- Inflammation of the middle ear (otitis interna) – usually as an extension of ear canker (see 'What if?' no.74).
- Aural haematoma – a hot and painful blood-filled swelling of the ear flap increasing slowly in size over a period of two to three days, probably accompanied by head shaking. This condition may be caused by a fight injury, or self-inflicted injury caused by aggressive scratching, or violent head shaking or banging, often associated with otitis externa. Veterinary help should be sought *at once*, as there is usually some underlying cause to make the dog injure its own ear and it is often necessary for the swelling to be drained surgically.
- Damage to the area of the brain controlling balance. If this is the case, the signs may also include unsteady gait, circling towards the affected side, involuntary movement of the eyes from side to side. If these signs are seen, consult your veterinary surgeon promptly so that the likely cause can be identified without delay.

What if my dog is breathing abnormally?

Panting enables a dog to cool itself by breathing hot air out over its extended tongue.

76

Dogs breathe through the nose when at rest, but through the mouth when running. Panting enables the dog to lose heat by blowing out hot air over the extended tongue.

Deep compulsive panting when at rest is a sign of nervous apprehension, e.g. when in a veterinary waiting room, or pain in the abdomen.

Abnormal breathing is also associated with five important emergency situations:

- Gastric dilation and torsion – see 'What if?' no.88.
- Heat stroke – see below.
- Airway obstruction – see below.
- Eclampsia (lactation tetany) – see page 97.
- Chest injury – see below.

Heat stroke – Cause: Over-exposure to heat which occurs classically in dogs confined in a closed car left parked in full sun. Short-nosed dogs, e.g. Boxers and Pekingese, are particularly prone. May also be seen in dogs with heavy, long coats that have been over-exercised or which have become

If a drowned dog can be easily lifted, swing it upside down (as illustrated below) to clear water from the lungs. Otherwise lie it on its side, pull its tongue forward and press on its chest intermittently.

over-excited in warm weather, especially if the humidity is high.

Signs: Excessive panting, restlessness, drooling and distress initially. As the dog's temperature rises further (it may reach as much as 43°C/110°F), the dog will radiate heat and feel very hot to the touch. These signs are followed by unconsciousness and collapse, the dog then rapidly becomes comatose and soon dies.

Treatment: It is vital to *cool the dog's body as rapidly as possible* by whatever means that are available. Thoroughly soak the dog with cold water, using buckets or a hose pipe, cover the dog's head and body with towels and blankets soaked in cold water, dunk the dog in a stream, use ice or even packs of frozen food. Care needs to be taken to keep the dog's airway clear. Ten minutes of cold water application should suffice – too much cooling can be counter-productive. As soon as the dog begins to recover, it should be taken to a veterinary surgeon without delay. This needs to be done even if the dog appears to be fully recovered since it may need to be given an intravenous drip and other medication to counteract shock.

Airway obstruction – Cause: Possible causes include swallowed tongue, foreign bodies such as a ball or pebble becoming lodged in the back of the throat, pharangeal swelling, and inhaled water following drowning.

Signs: Strenuous respiratory efforts with the animal gasping for breath and, if the airway is only partially blocked, breathing much more rapidly. The affected dog will usually lie on its chest with its head and neck extended. Initially it will lie still but if the airway remains occluded the dog will throw itself about, its gums will go blue and death will ensue very rapidly.

Treatment: Try to remove the cause as soon as possible to clear the dog's airway. If drowning is the cause and the dog is small enough to lift, swing it head downwards by its hind legs to drain ▶

Note: With all breathing problems, it is better to seek veterinary advice early, than regret not doing so later.

the fluid in the lungs and airway quickly, give chest massage and, if the dog stops breathing altogether, give mouth to nose resuscitation by breathing up the dog's nose while holding its mouth shut (see page 69). *Rush to the nearest veterinary surgery*, contacting the vet by mobile phone on the way.

Note: Pinching hard between a dog's nostrils when it has stopped breathing can sometimes stimulate it to take a gasp and to start breathing again. Vigorous towelling of the dog's body can also be of help in many cases.

Chest injury The cause is most frequently a fall, road traffic accident, or fight with a larger dog. In all cases transport your dog gently and carefully to a veterinary surgery without delay.

What if my dog is shedding hair?

77

All dogs, with a few exceptions (e.g. Poodles and Bedlington Terriers), shed dead hair from the coat. Sometimes the shedding is seasonal, but some heavy coated dogs which originated in cold climates, for instance Labradors, shed all the year round if they are kept in a warm house. When a dog has started to moult, it is best to give it a thorough grooming out of doors to remove all the dead coat and allow the new hair to grow. German Shepherd Dogs and other dogs with a dense undercoat shed large amounts of hair in the spring. Be prepared for this normal occurrence. Some other conditions associated with hair loss are:

- After whelping and lactation in some bitches.
- After infection/chronic infections.
- Old age.
- Poor or unsuitable diet.
- Acute digestive problems or allergies.
- Hormonal imbalance. Hair loss is quite often associated with an hormonal imbalance or deficiency, e.g. in some spayed bitches and dogs with a thyroid deficiency. In such cases the hair loss is usually in large patches on the side of the neck or on the flanks and it frequently

German Shepherd Dogs have a thick undercoat; owners must expect prolific hair shedding in the spring.

occurs as symmetrical areas on both sides of the body. A veterinary examination, possibly including the examination of a blood sample, may be necessary to pinpoint the cause so that effective treatment can be given.

What if my dog is scratching excessively?

78

Dogs, like humans, scratch because they are itching (pruritus). Persistent scratching should not be allowed to continue. The main cause of the itching is parasites in the coat biting, sucking and causing damage to the skin. The parasites most commonly involved are fleas, lice, cheyletiella (the rabbit fur mite) and sarcoptic mange mites. Although dogs suffering from sarcoptic mange scratch frantically, dogs with demodectic mange, surprisingly, do not scratch excessively.

Other cases of scratching include inflammatory conditions of the skin (dermatitis) caused principally by allergies (the allergens may gain entry to the body through inhalation, ingestion or by contact with the skin), or bacterial infection. In some cases fungal infections may be involved and in others autoimmune disease or neuroses may be the root cause of the irritation leading to excessive scratching.

Ixodes ricinus is a parasitic hard tick that can infest dogs.

Diagnosis: Parasite Infection is probably the major cause of skin disease in dogs. However, because the signs are not specific to any one cause veterinary help should be sought if any skin lesions or signs of skin irritation are shown by dogs, so that a proper diagnosis of the cause can be made and the most effective treatment prescribed. This often involves the microscopic examination of skin scrapings. It is helpful to have to hand a good history of the case, noting details of the signs shown, their time of onset and duration and whether they are affected by particular events, surroundings or dietary changes. Details relating to the dog's environment – particularly the bedding used and possible contact with other animals – can also help diagnosis. Finally, it is important to inform the veterinary surgeon if any person in contact with affected dogs is also showing signs of skin disease. All this information will help the vet to select the most cost-effective product and advise about the most appropriate treatment regime. ▶

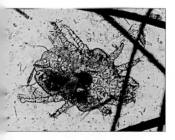

The cheyletiella mite (above) causes white scaling on the fur (above right), particularly on the back and flanks.

FLEAS

It makes sense to inspect your dog regularly for the presence of fleas. If you do find fleas or any flea excrement, it is important to take action at once to control them on your dog and, just as importantly, in your house and car. Otherwise you may create a hatchery of fleas that will be with you for a long time. Furthermore flea control is important since your dog could become sensitive to flea bites and the resulting skin condition can be time-consuming and costly to cure. Indeed in some cases it may only be possible to control the skin rash on a temporary basis and permanent medication may be required. Flea bite dermatitis is one of the most common skin problems in dogs nowadays. It has become especially significant recently, probably because many more houses have central heating.

Adult flea

Pupae

Larvae

Eggs

Adult fleas lay eggs which develop into larvae and then into pupae. Pupae hatch into fleas only when the ambient conditions are right.

Signs: Look for small, flattened, brown, elongated, wingless insects. They run over the dog's skin through the hair and jump when they are off the animal; they may be difficult to spot in dogs that groom themselves meticulously. Look particularly around the neck and at the base of the tail. If you think fleas may be present but you can't find evidence, see your vet. He or she will probably comb the dog and look for the black flea dirts, which are only

Modern sprays and 'spot on' treatments are available to control fleas. The latter can kill adult fleas as well as their eggs, larvae and pupae.

FLEAS – THE ESSENTIAL FACTS

- It is a myth that fleas exist only where there's dirt and disease. Central heating and carpeting provide an environment where fleas thrive.
- Adult fleas spend virtually all their life on their host. The intermediate stages in the flea's life cycle, larvae and pupae, develop in crevices in the house, in furnishings, between floorboards and around the edge of fitted carpets.
- In their lifetime female fleas can lay as many as 400-500 eggs which can be seen with the naked eye. The eggs develop into larvae and then pupae which can remain dormant for up to a year before hatching into adult fleas. Hatching is triggered by some vibration in association with the right conditions of temperature and humidity.
- Dogs can pick up tapeworms by swallowing fleas.

A flea larva emerging from an egg. Larvae shun light and so tend to live in dark places like the edges of the carpet where they feed on organic debris.

An adult female flea can lay up to 50 eggs a day (below). In the course of a day it may ingest up to 15 times its own weight in blood.

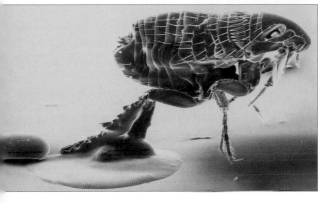

the size of grains of sand, and which leave a tell-tale reddish-brown mark when placed on damp blotting paper. In dogs that are hypersensitive to flea bites there may be a simple rash on the abdomen but in severe cases the skin on the back becomes thickened, folded and darkly coloured.

Treatment: Talk to your vet, who will advise which products ('spot ons', sprays, insecticidal collars or oral medication) are most appropriate in your case. Be sure to ask how frequently they should be used to ensure that existing fleas are killed and to prevent re-infection.

Prevention: A number of very effective products are also available for use around the home. Many contain a short-acting insecticide, which will kill any adult fleas that are present and a longer-acting compound which will prevent flea eggs hatching and larvae maturing into adults, thus breaking the whole life cycle. They can give up to seven months' protection when used as directed. Your vet will advise the most cost effective anti-flea campaign for your circumstances.

LICE

Life cycle: Adult lice (scientific name *Trichodectes canis*) feed on the skin and lay eggs on the hair. These hatch into young lice which resemble the adults. Lice cannot exist off their host for more than a few days; infection is spread, therefore, by close contact between animals.

Signs: Adult lice are light brown, fat, wingless insects with short legs that move slowly on the skin surface and which lay eggs (nits) that stick to the animal's hair, particularly around the neck and ears. Dogs with lice will scratch frequently at the area where the insects are to be found. Severe infections may cause anaemia in young puppies.

Treatment: Regular treatment of infected dogs with an insecticide is required and it makes sense to comb and wash away the nits. Since lice only live and breed on an animal, there is less need to pay attention to the environment than is the case with flea infection.

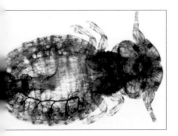

An adult specimen of the louse Trichodectes canis.

What if my dog keeps breaking wind?

79

Breaking wind, stomach rumbling and flatulence are not usually associated with any specific major disease, and seldom seem to trouble the dog, although they often cause considerable social embarrassment to the owner. Some possible causes are noted in the table below.

POSSIBLE CAUSES OF FLATULENCE

Cause	Action
Unsuitable diet, e.g. damaged foodstuffs, possibly a diet low in fibre but may also be associated with a diet high in fibre.	Take advice about obtaining more easily digested food.
Sudden diet change.	Dietary changes should be made gradually over at least four to five days.
Feeding household leftovers – highly seasoned and spiced foods can create digestive problems in dogs.	Feeding such foods should be avoided.
Scavenging – dogs are attracted to the smell of decaying flesh and will eat putrid carcasses.	Keep the dog under stricter control and dispose of uneaten food carefully in a closed waste bin.
Constipation.	The addition of 10 per cent bran to the diet may help. A special commercial diet may be needed. Your vet will advise.
Old age. Lack of muscle tone in the digestive tract and a reduced ability to digest protein, fat and carbohydrate.	Try giving four small easily digested meals a day. Your veterinary surgeon may advise you to use a commercially manufactured diet especially formulated for elderly dogs.

Breaking wind and flatulence may also be associated with pancreatic deficiency and other general digestive upsets, especially those causing diarrhoea.

A number of special diets are available through veterinary surgeons. It is always wise to consult your veterinary surgeon about your dog's diet when you visit for other reasons, as a dog's dietary needs vary through its lifetime. An appropriate adjustment to your dog's diet could give it a new lease of life and increase its lifespan.

What if my dog is biting its tail, scooting or rubbing its bottom on the ground?

80

This behaviour is common in dogs and it is nearly always due to anal gland problems. The popular notion that worm infestation is the principal cause of irritation around the anus is generally unfounded, but if this sign is caused by worms, you will see small worm segments, like grains of rice, around your dog's anus.

The anal glands, situated on either side of the anus, should empty every time faeces are passed, depositing their contents on the faeces as a scent marker. This was useful to the wild or wandering dog, but is largely obsolete for the household pet. A diet containing more bulk may serve to make the anal glands empty more regularly.

Anal glands which become overfull and which are not relieved manually may become infected by bacteria causing an abscess which can burst causing an evil-smelling wound. This condition can be prevented by having the anal glands emptied periodically at the veterinary surgery. In skilled hands this service is quickly performed and needs no anaesthetic. The anal glands can be removed surgically if trouble persists.

Dogs typically perform this scooting action when they have problems with their anal glands. Worms may also give rise to a sore rear end.

Some other conditions which may cause these signs are:

Anal furunculosis – sore skin around the anus with open wounds discharging pus; the cause is unknown but is possibly due to an abnormal immune response. This condition is almost exclusive to German Shepherd Dogs and Belgian Shepherd Dogs.

Anal adenomata – lumps (benign tumours) around the anus which can become raw and ulcerated through pressure, licking and contact with the ground. *Seek veterinary advice at once* as the area is unlikely to heal naturally.

What if my dog has diarrhoea?

81 Diarrhoea is defined as the more frequent passing of liquid faeces. It is always worthwhile taking note of the frequency with which your dog passes faeces normally and their consistency, colour and amount, so as to be aware of any changes that may occur. It is normal for an adult dog to pass faeces once or twice daily, but three times daily can be regarded as normal. Puppies frequently defecate as much as four to six times daily. Diarrhoea is commonly associated with many illnesses, some relatively trivial, but some of a serious nature.

Some possible causes of diarrhoea which a veterinary surgeon will consider are:

- Dietary – sudden dietary change, excess or low fibre in the diet, overfeeding in young puppies, damaged foods, carbohydrate intolerance or food hypersensitivity. Some specific foods that have been incriminated are liver and offal, raw eggs, onions and too much milk (e.g. more than 570ml/1 pint for a Labrador-sized dog).

Persistent diarrhoea in puppies is a serious concern – seek prompt advice from your vet .

- Bacterial infections.
- Viral infections.
- Parasite infections.
- Poisons – particularly plant and some metallic poisons.
- Functional – partial obstruction of the bowel and tumours of the colon.
- Enzyme deficiencies – particularly pancreatic insufficiency.
- Diarrhoea may occasionally be associated with stress, particularly in dogs with a nervous temperament.

First Aid Treatment

- Withhold food for 12 hours.
- Water must always be freely supplied; diarrhoea cannot be 'dried up' by withholding water.
- Begin feeding again using scrambled eggs, or fish, with plain boiled rice. Feed in small quantities several times a day.

If diarrhoea persists, or if there are other signs of illness, contact a veterinary surgeon *without delay*, since it may be caused by a number of infections and other factors (described above). Diarrhoea merits even earlier veterinary consultation in young puppies, as they quickly become dehydrated.

Note: Bitches that eat large numbers of afterbirths when whelping may have diarrhoea temporarily.

What if my dog is passing blood in its faeces?

82 Occasional, very slight streaks of fresh blood on the outside of the stool are likely to come from a small broken blood vessel around the anus and are unimportant provided the dog is otherwise well. However, if even this small amount of blood is seen persistently, veterinary advice should be sought. Digested blood from the throat, stomach or small intestine produces a black stool. There may be streaks of fresh red blood on the faeces in conditions where the lower bowel is damaged. If a dessertspoonful (10-15ml) or more of fresh red blood is passed with the faeces, *your veterinary surgeon should be consulted immediately* as this sign is associated with some major canine diseases, particularly canine parvovirus infection; it may also occur in cases of poisoning.

Polyps in the rectum which sometimes protrude may cause constipation or straining and can be a cause of blood-stained faeces. Although they are unlikely to be malignant, a veterinary surgeon should be consulted about their removal.

What if my dog is constipated?

Many instances of constipation can be relieved by administering medicinal liquid paraffin.

83 Constipation is not uncommon, especially in toy breeds. However, if constipation persists or the dog is obviously in pain, then veterinary attention should be sought quite promptly.

Some common simple causes of constipation:
- Low residue, all meat diet.
- Feeding bones which can be crunched up.
- Dogs confined indoors all day; insufficient exercise.
- Travelling long distances by car so that the dog has no chance to relieve itself as normal.
- Matted fur beneath tail.

First Aid Treatment Where constipation is associated with the causes listed above, medicinal liquid paraffin may be given at the dose of one dessertspoon for a 30lb dog (10ml per 13.5kg dog), and pro rata for other weights. Giving too great a quantity is not harmful but the excess will probably leak from the anus.

Some other relatively common causes of constipation and straining to pass faeces include:
- Enlarged prostate gland in older male dogs (see page 96).
- Stricture (narrowing of the rectum). This is sometimes congenital, but is more often caused by straining to pass a sharp object like splinters of bone. Stools may be passed but only after considerable straining, and they may contain a little fresh red blood. Seek veterinary advice *without delay*.

What if my dog is not passing urine, or is straining to pass small amounts frequently?

84 Not passing urine may be a voluntary decision on the dog's part. Bitches in particular are capable of withholding urine for as long as 24 hours when off their home territory.

In all other circumstances, failure to pass urine or difficulty in doing so (urinary tenesmus) is always a serious emergency and should certainly not be neglected if it continues for more than 24 hours. Be prepared to consult your veterinary surgeon earlier if other signs, such as lack or appetite or vomiting, are present. The pain of a full bladder which cannot be emptied is agonizing.

Some technical causes of urinary tenesmus that a veterinary surgeon will consider are inflammation of the urinary bladder (cystitis), inflammation of the urethra, bladder stones (urolithiasis), urethral or vaginal tumours and possibly prostatic disease in dogs.

What if my dog is incontinent?

One of the most annoying examples of incontinence is the very submissive bitch which dribbles urine when excited or when greeting people. For information on this condition see page 26.

85 A distinction must be made between the puppy or adult which is not successfully house-trained and true incontinence, which is the dripping of urine without the dog being aware of it. It is rare that a dog cannot be house-trained, but in some individuals it has proved impossible. Likewise, territory marking by male dogs and bitches on heat should not be confused with incontinence.

During illness and in extreme old age overnight incontinence is not unusual. Such dogs can be kept clean and comfortable by making up a bed on a sheet of plastic topped with thickly spread newspaper over which is laid a polyester fur rug which allows urine to pass through rather than making the rug wet. Arthritic dogs may also have difficulty in rising from bed to urinate, especially first thing in the morning, and thus they may have 'accidents'.

Incontinence is not an uncommon sequel to spaying, especially in large bitches and when the operation is performed on young puppies or on middle-aged or older bitches. Such cases can sometimes be treated with hormone medication – your vet will advise; the condition may need to be corrected surgically. Incontinence in young puppies may be associated with a congenital defect in the urinary system which can often be corrected

Don't be angry if your elderly dog is incontinent around the house; it is an involuntary act of which the animal is not aware.

surgically. If your puppy drips urine constantly day and night, seek veterinary help promptly.

Incontinence is also associated with paralysis and with inflammation of the bladder (cystitis) or stones in the bladder. Any disease which causes excessive drinking will also lead to the more frequent passage of urine, see 'What if?' no.69.

Incontinence is not itself a serious sign since there are many simple causes, such as over-submissiveness, as noted. However, if other signs are present or if the dog shows discomfort or pain on passing urine, or if the urine contains blood, it is wise to seek veterinary help without delay (see also 'What if?' no.86).

What if my dog is passing blood in its urine?

86

Bitches: It is normal for a bitch on heat or a newly whelped bitch to have a bloodstained discharge from the vulva which will blend with the urine. In any other circumstances blood in the urine (haematuria) is a serious sign, so *a veterinary surgeon should be consulted as soon as possible*. It is helpful and saves time to take a urine sample with you.

Note whether blood is present every time the bitch urinates and whether it is present in the first or last urine to be passed, or generally mixed with it. Record too whether the urine is passed with difficulty and whether or not urination is associated with pain before, during or after urine is passed.

Other causes of blood in the urine that a veterinary surgeon will consider are stones in the urinary bladder, cystitis, growths and tumours, trauma to the urinary tract and infection, specifically leptospirosis.

Dogs: Blood in the urine of dogs may be associated with stones in the bladder or urethra, cystitis, growths and tumours (although rarely), trauma (possibly following a road traffic accident), kidney disease and prostate disease.

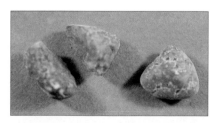

These bladder stones are composed of crystals of struvite; uroliths like this are a common cause of blood showing in the urine.

Septicaemia, toxaemia or warfarin poisoning may cause blood to be passed in the urine in both dogs and bitches. Because of the great number and variety of causes, *it is sensible always to seek veterinary attention if your pet's urine contains blood*.

What if my dog has a discharge from its penis or vulva (or licks excessively at its genitals)?

87 It is normal for male dogs to have a small amount of whitish, mucoid discharge from the prepuce (the skin covering the top of the penis), and bitch puppies also often have a drop of mucus on the vulva.

It is common dog behaviour for both sexes to pay attention to cleaning the genital area. Bitches coming into season will pay extra attention to the vulva, and they will also do this after whelping.

An excessive amount of or a foul-smelling discharge, the presence of lesions on the genitals, or an obsession with licking them is abnormal and such dogs should be taken to a veterinary surgeon so that the cause can be diagnosed – possibly, in dogs, inflammation of the sheath covering the penis (balanitis) or inflammation of the sheath and the penis itself (balanoposthitis). **Note:** A copious discharge of foul-smelling, blood-stained fluid from the vulva also occurs in cases of open pyometra (see page 98). See also 'What if?' no.111.

What if my dog is pot-bellied?

88 It is normal for young puppies to show considerable abdominal distension after eating but if the expansion is gross, consideration should be given to spreading the food intake over more frequent, but smaller, meals. Adult dogs showing this sign may also benefit from being fed two or more smaller meals a day, especially when high bulk, complete dry diets are used.

A pot-bellied puppy which is thin on the shoulders and hindquarters, with poor coat is possibly suffering from a worm infection (see page 100). However, rather than assuming that is the problem and purchasing a worming remedy, it is sensible to seek veterinary attention. The vet will recommend the most effective remedy and give advice on administration, particularly

Don't confuse a bit of middle-age spread (below) with a pot-bellied appearance. A pot belly is distended in a way that is out of proportion with the rest of the body.

the frequency of dosing after having confirmed, by examination of a faeces sample, that the problem is indeed caused by a worm infection.

The most common cause of serious abdominal enlargement in adult dogs is:

A sudden enlargement of the abdomen after eating is not a good sign; pay close attention to your dog as bloat may be the culprit, especially in the case of large dogs.

Gastric dilation and torsion (bloat) This is a sudden enlargement of the stomach which is usually full of fermenting food and gas. The condition is complicated when the stomach twists, blocking both the entrance from the throat and the exit to the small intestines. Dogs of 18kg (40lb) weight and upwards are most usually affected.

Signs: A sudden and noticeable enlargement of the abdomen, usually soon after eating. The condition is seen particularly in deep-chested breeds that are greedy eaters. The dog is in great pain and distress, and has difficulty in breathing. There may be an attempt to vomit and pass faeces, but when torsion (twisting) has taken place nothing can pass. The affected dog becomes listless and shows signs of shock and cries in pain.

Cause: No definitive cause has been found. Suspicion has fallen on violent exercise after feeding, copious drinking on top of dry meals, blockage of the stomach exit by indigestible material, excess fermentation in the stomach and overloading the stomach with one large meal eaten quickly.

Accumulation of fluid in the abdominal cavity (ascites) can be associated with heart or liver disease. It causes noticeable distension of the abdomen, as seen here.

Action: *This is one of the true veterinary emergencies*. Releasing the gas and emptying the stomach by mechanical means is imperative as this condition can rapidly be fatal. It is also important to combat the life-threatening circulatory collapse that is associated with the condition. *Make contact with a veterinary surgeon at once, day or night, and be prepared to drive the dog to the surgery immediately*.

Prevention: Your vet will advise you about the preventive measures which may help to avoid a recurrence of the condition, particularly feeding a more moist diet and giving more frequent, smaller meals, possibly from bowls placed at a raised level.

Other causes of pot-bellied appearance which are not due to overfeeding are heart disease, accumulation of fluid in the abdominal cavity (ascites), pregnancy and false pregnancy, pyometra, some hormone disorders and other major abdominal diseases which are accompanied by fluid retention.

What if my dog is limping?

89

Dogs limp because of pain or a 'mechanical' problem with a leg. A dog may often take the weight off an injured foreleg when standing still and, when moving, may nod or drop the head as the weight goes onto the opposite foreleg. Similarly the hindquarters will be dropped when the sound hindleg is placed on the ground. If a dog is holding its leg off the ground, the problem is most likely to be in the foot. If it places its foot gently to the ground or drags the leg, the injury is likely to be higher up.

Very often the cause of an acute limp is easily diagnosed. Look at the foot to detect impaled thorns, stone chippings, balls of tar, or snow wedged between the pads, which are common causes of limping in dogs.

Examine the rest of the leg for signs of injury, such as swelling, deformity, pain, loss of function or a break in the skin. In most cases it is sensible to seek veterinary advice promptly but if the dog is otherwise well, is eating, and the pain is not severe, then such action can be delayed for 24 hours. Other causes of limping are:

Arthritis Many new very effective products are available to vets which can ease the pain, but continual medication may be needed. In some cases, surgery may be required.

Bone fractures Usually the result of road traffic accidents or falls, causing sudden severe pain and inability to put weight on the leg which may be visibly deformed. Contact a vet *quickly* for diagnosis and fixation. Repair these days is usually good.

Dislocations The displacement through accidental injury of one or more bones which form a joint. The hip and shoulder joints are most frequently affected. Veterinary consultation is needed *at once* as there may be internal bleeding into the joint cavity or an associated fracture. Generally, correction of a dislocation is more likely to be successful if it is carried out without delay.

Sprains Damage to the ligaments or tendons supporting the joint by being overstretched or torn through wrenching or twisting. Initially as a first aid measure put a cold compress on the affected joint without delay, using ice or a pack of frozen food, to reduce the swelling and pain. Prompt veterinary consultation is necessary to assess the extent of the damage and commence treatment.

Strains Damage to the muscles. Muscles are most often torn or damaged by a sudden wrench or twisting movement, particularly in racing dogs. Action as for sprains – see above. Subsequently

Dogs that walk up to you on three legs while holding one foot in the air often have a foreign object impaled in that paw or something wedged between the pads.

complete rest of the limb and prompt veterinary advice for differential diagnosis and further treatment.

Inflamed swellings between the toes Some dogs are subject to a succession of these swellings (interdigital cysts) which occur mostly on the front feet. The cause is thought to lie principally in the sweat glands in the foot but in some cases they may be associated with congenital ingrowing hairs between the toes or physical or chemical irritants. The cysts may become infected by bacteria and quite often contain grass seeds. Cysts on the top of the foot often rupture spontaneously. Affected dogs show lameness, a red swollen area between the toes on the upper side of the paw, continual licking of the site and often brown staining of the hair. A veterinary consultation is needed promptly for immediate treatment and future prevention, which may involve lancing and long-term treatment with antibiotics.

What if my dog is coughing?

90 It is normal for a dog to cough occasionally, particularly after a bout of barking, or after vigorous play. Any dog which suddenly begins to cough persistently should be segregated from other dogs, kept very quiet and taken to a veterinary surgeon promptly. Even if the cough is occasional and not severe, if it persists for more than a week the cause should be investigated. Coughing is associated with the following major diseases and conditions:

- Canine distemper
- Kennel cough
- Heart disease
- Respiratory disease

Other possible causes of coughing include:

- Bronchitis – from breathing in irritants or an allergic reaction. If sudden and severe, telephone a veterinary surgeon for advice on first aid treatment.
- Injury to the chest, possibly as the result of a road traffic accident.
- Pharyngitis, laryngitis and tonsillitis. Remember that tonsillitis is often an early sign of a major infectious disease and it should not be treated lightly. Some breeds of dog seem especially susceptible to recurrent bouts of tonsillitis and surgical removal of the tonsils may be advocated.

Persistent coughing is often a sign of a serious illness. Don't ignore it – see your vet.

129

What if my dog is eating with difficulty?

Poorly maintained teeth can cause a dog to experience eating difficulties.

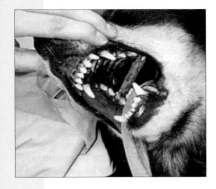

This dog has a piece of stick wedged between its upper carnassial teeth. Veterinary help will be needed.

91 Decaying teeth and gum disease are common causes of difficulty in eating. The study and practice of veterinary dentistry is advancing all the time and much can be done to minimize pain and avoid the need for tooth extraction. Seek veterinary advice promptly if in doubt – see also 'What if?' no.92.

Other causes of difficulty in eating include:

Growths and tumours in the mouth (neoplasia) Arrange a veterinary consultation as soon as possible with a view to removal of the growth. Treatment can be very successful.

Foreign body lodged in mouth The signs include sudden onset of foul breath, gagging, retching, drooling or foaming at the mouth, pawing and rubbing the mouth. Typically, a piece of bone or stick gets lodged across the roof of the mouth, between the upper carnassial teeth, cotton or string gets wound round the teeth or an elastic band fixed on the dog's tongue. It is best not to persist in trying to remove the obstruction, if it does not come away easily, take the dog to the veterinary surgery. A sedative may be needed while the obstruction is removed.

Broken teeth From time to time dog's teeth break, often because they are encouraged to catch hard balls or even stones. Initially a broken tooth is likely to be painful to the touch but once the nerve is dead the pain subsides. However an abscess often subsequently develops inside the jawbone leading to more pain. It is advisable to seek professional help if your dog breaks a tooth.

Crooked teeth Most of the irregularities of a dog's bite are inherited and correcting the problem will not prevent them being passed to future generations. Such abnormalities seldom cause the dog much of a problem.

Retained milk teeth Sometimes milk teeth are not lost at the correct time and this may divert the permanent teeth into a poor position. Your veterinary surgeon will advise whether removal of temporary teeth that are not shed is necessary.

What if my dog has bad breath?

92 Mild cases of bad breath are often associated with what the dog eats – for example, lots of fish. Scavenging will also render the breath unpleasant. The mouth harbours many naturally occurring bacteria which can form a film on the teeth and infect the gap between the teeth and the gums leading to the formation of plaque. This can then calcify to form tartar – hard deposits on the teeth (calculus). It is the activity of the bacterial deposits that leads to mouth odour.

Many owners think that providing bones will help keep their pet's teeth clean. This is a fallacy and can be harmful as chewing bones can lead to broken teeth, penetration of the digestive tract and constipation. Rawhide chews and some of the treats designed especially for the purpose can help to prevent inflammation of the gums (gingivitis). Consult your vet or the nurse so that the most appropriate product for your dog's needs can be obtained.

Brushing your dog's teeth two or three times a week can help keep its mouth and gums clean and healthy. Toothpaste and toothbrushes specially designed for dogs are available and products containing chlorhexidine are considered the best. Don't use human toothpaste as it is too frothy and strongly flavoured for animals. They cannot spit it out, and swallowing it can upset their digestion.

Never use salt or baking soda as this can be fatal, especially for an older animal with a heart condition.

Where the odour is persistent and very noticeable, it is wise to have the dog examined by a veterinary surgeon.

Other possible causes of bad breath include:

Inflammation of the gums Inflammation of the gums is associated with the accumulation of tartar deposits (periodontal disease). This is by far the most common cause of loss of teeth in dogs. Regular tooth brushing and possibly visits to the veterinary surgeon for scaling can be enormously beneficial for the dog's health and comfort. Feeding hard, crunchy food and using special dog chews can help prevent the condition occurring.

Foreign body lodged in mouth See 'What if?' no.91.

Tooth decay This is characterized by difficulty in eating, possibly swelling and abscess formation over the root of the tooth. The upper carnassial tooth is most often affected and leads to a swelling on the cheek, often called a facial abscess, just below and in front of the eye. This can burst, leaving a discharging painful sinus. While it is sometimes possible to fill teeth which are decayed, it is hardly practical, and painful teeth are usually extracted under anaesthesia by a vet.

Bad breath may also be associated with some major diseases, e.g. kidney disease and liver disease.

It pays to brush your dog's teeth at least once a week to maintain good dental hygiene. Specially formulated toothpaste and 'finger' brushes like the one illustrated below are readily available.

131

What if my dog is having fits, convulsions or is twitching?

93 It is normal for newly born puppies to twitch frequently when resting and older dogs may twitch and whimper during their sleep while dreaming. A true fit, however, is a convulsive seizure occurring typically while the dog is relaxed or asleep and not while the dog is active. A fit usually begins with a period of rigidity (tonic phase) which is followed by a shaking and spasm of the muscles, which progresses to involuntary paddling with the paws (clonic phase). There may be involuntary passing of faeces and urine. The fit may last only a minute or two and the dog may recover quickly and appear perfectly normal. In other cases the fit may be more prolonged and the dog may appear dazed and disorientated for some hours after the convulsions have stopped. Sight seems to be the last sense to return fully to a recovering dog. Dogs often eat ravenously after a fit. In severe episodes, one fit may lead very quickly to several more.

Although it is unlikely that the dog will harm humans or itself while in a fit, it is wise to be cautious. While the fit lasts, do not touch the dog, but remove anything lying nearby which could cause it injury and gently move the dog by using a blanket if it is lying in a dangerous place, such as the top of the stairs. Turn off radios and the TV and keep the room dark and quiet. It is wise to report the incident to the vet. The causes of fits include:

Epilepsy This condition often occurs for the first time at around two years of age. It is a quite a common condition in dogs, but can often be controlled by medication so that the affected dog can enjoy a full lifespan. Fits are caused by abnormal electrical discharges in the brain. Their origin is unknown but there may be a predisposition associated with a number of factors such as age, sex, heredity, drugs or oestrus. Since fits may sometimes be associated with brain tumours, previous trauma, inherited conditions such as water on the brain (hydrocephalus), canine distemper and liver disease or eclampsia, always seek veterinary attention since an accurate diagnosis of the cause is essential before any medication is given. If the fits are to be controlled effectively, the directions given by your vet must be followed precisely and consistently. Properly controlled medication can allow affected dogs to live quite normally.

Rabies Where this disease is endemic, rabies needs to be considered as a possible cause of fitting. Special precautions will need to be taken if the affected dog has recently returned from an area where rabies is present in the wildlife. Your vet will advise you of the procedures that need to be followed in this case.

There is no point in asking the veterinary surgeon to make an urgent visit to a dog which is having a fit, as it will almost certainly be normal by the time help is obtained. Once the dog has recovered from the fit, report to the veterinary surgeon by telephone for advice and arrange for a full veterinary 'check up'.

What if my dog has a lump or swelling?

94

Any lumps and swellings which do not begin to subside or disappear within a few days should be investigated by a vet. This is particularly important for the early recognition of abscesses and tumours.

Causes of lumps or swellings include, commonly:

Abscess A swelling beneath the skin caused by bacterial infection. Often the result of a bite or puncture wound, frequently as a result of a fight with a cat. The signs include pain, heat and swelling, possibly accompanied by raised body temperature (fever) developing over a few days. The swellings usually subsequently burst and discharge pus. Abscesses may occur anywhere on the body. Contact the veterinary surgeon promptly as the condition may need surgical drainage and medication with antibiotics is frequently required.

Painful swellings between the toes See 'What if?' no.89.

Warts and papillomas These are painless dark-coloured projections from the skin (tags) that are usually small. The cause is unknown but may possibly involve a viral infection. Seek veterinary advice if the wart is increasing in size rapidly, otherwise mention the wart at the next routine consultation. Spontaneous recovery is quite common. Warts may be removed surgically, by cryotherapy, or the use of special topical applications.

Blood-filled swelling (haematoma) A swelling resulting from an injury to blood vessels or to drainage of fluid post-operatively. The ear flap is a common site – see also 'What if?' no.75. A haematoma presents as a soft swelling and distortion of the area – sometimes painful to the touch, but not usually so. Nor is it usually associated with raised body temperature or loss of appetite. Consult your vet promptly as surgical treatment may be required.

Stings and insect bites Evidenced by a sudden swelling which may be severe, and dangerous if the face and mouth is affected, especially in short-nosed breeds. Remove the sting with tweezers if it can be seen. Use an anti-sting stick and/or swab the area with surgical spirit or distilled witch hazel. Contact your veterinary surgeon *immediately* if breathing or swallowing is impaired, if your dog appears to be in great pain, or if it develops a severe allergic reaction and shows signs of shock and collapse.

Lumps and swellings may also be associated with itchy raised wheals on the skin (urticaria) and possibly tumours, the most common being mammary tumours – see page 99. If these conditions are suspected, seek veterinary help.

Large breeds quite commonly develop swellings on their elbows or hocks; this risk can be minimized by ensuring that the dog has an adequate number of soft areas where it can lie and rest.

The large swelling on this dog's face and neck was caused by an adder bite. Insect stings can also cause quite severe allergic reactions.

What if my dog is wounded, grazed, cut, burnt or scalded?

95

Action: Minor wounds and grazes

Allow the dog to lick and cleanse the area but be careful that it, or any companion animals, do not lick the wound excessively. This can be prevented by distracting the dog and teaching it not to lick or by bandaging. For certain wounds, and where bandaging is difficult, it may be necessary to apply a wide collar (an Elizabethan collar) around the dog's neck to prevent it getting at the wound – your veterinary surgeon will advise and, if necessary, provide one of the correct size for your dog.

If the dog cannot reach the wound or is not licking itself, cleanse the wound with salt water (one tablespoon in 285ml/half a pint), and/or dilute antiseptic (e.g. TCP). Subsequently apply a small amount of antiseptic cream or ointment. This treatment should be repeated two to three times daily until healing has occurred.

Action: Severe wounds

Seeping dark blood indicates that a vein has probably been severed. Clean the wound as above and apply a pad of lint (woven side to the wound) or a strip of bandage, cover with a layer of damp cotton wool and bandage with a woven cotton bandage or a crepe bandage. Be careful not to apply the bandage too tightly. Check at regular intervals that swelling is not occurring below the bandage. Remove the bandage daily, dress the wound, apply an antiseptic ointment or cream, and re-bandage until healing takes place or is well on the way. A piece of woven tubular bandage (Tubigauze) may be used to help keep bandages in place.

Foot bandages may be kept clean by putting the dog's paw in an old sock which can be covered with a polythene bag when the dog goes outside. It is best to tape the sock and bag in place with

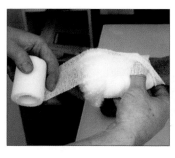

Cuts to the legs can be treated by winding an open-weave bandage around a pad of lint or cotton wool.

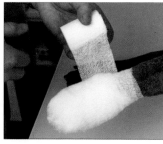

This dressing is secured by taking a number of turns around the leg. Take care not to wind it too tightly.

Finally adhesive sticking plaster is applied to hold the entire bandage securely in place.

SENSIBLE PRECAUTIONS

- It is important to ensure that hair is not getting into the wound – this may necessitate clipping around the edge of the wound with blunt-ended curved-on-flat scissors.
- Deep puncture wounds can lead to abscess formation since they often heal too quickly on the surface leaving infection to brew under the skin. If your dog has been in a fight with a cat, it is wise to visit the surgery since antibiotic medication may be needed.
- If you have any doubts about the severity of a wound, or if during healing the edges are very inflamed and sore and the surrounding area feels hot to the touch, *seek veterinary advice without delay*.

Women's tights come in handy when you need to stop a wounded ear from flapping when the dog shakes its head.

sticking plaster rather than use an elastic band, since the latter can cause severe problems if left in place for too long and can easily be picked up by the dog and become fixed on its tongue.

If the area becomes excessively swollen, the wound smells, or pus is present, seek veterinary assistance. Antibiotic medication may be needed.

Bright red, spurting blood from a wound indicates that an artery has been severed. Provided that a large vessel is not involved, a pressure bandage applied as described above will usually suffice to control the haemorrhage. A second layer of cotton wool and bandage may be required if blood seeps through the first. Once the bleeding has stopped, treatment can continue the next day as described previously. If such methods fail to stop the bleeding, then a tourniquet will need to be applied at a suitable point between the heart and the wound. Do not leave tourniquets on for excessive periods; check by feeling the skin below the tourniquet – if it is cold and blue, the pressure must be released slightly. If it is necessary to apply a tourniquet, *veterinary help must be sought* since tying off (ligating) the artery may be required so that bleeding is controlled without adversely affecting the blood supply to the rest of the limb.

Deep cuts more than 2.5cm (1in) in length may need stitching. Seek veterinary help *without delay* since if the wound is repaired early the chances of it healing quickly are greatly increased.

Wounds in the pads or the ear flaps present special problems in that walking or shaking may well make the wound start to bleed again. Foot wounds may need suturing if deep and professional bandaging can save a lot of mess in the house. If an ear flap is cut, a length of Tubigauze, or a tube made from a leg from a pair of tights, can be placed over the dog's head for 12 to 24 hours to prevent the ear flapping when the head is shaken; the ear flaps should first be folded over each other on the top of the head.

What if my dog is licking itself excessively?

96 If a dog is seen to be licking excessively at one area of the body, check for some unsuspected injury, insect sting/bite or a thorn embedded in the flesh. Continual licking can cause additional damage to the skin and so should be investigated.

Excessive licking may cause a chronic skin abrasion called a lick granuloma. This is usually a self-inflicted injury often resulting from boredom, frustration or nervousness. The condition appears as a sore, thickened, red area of skin in a place the dog can reach easily, frequently on the front of the wrist (carpus). Seek veterinary advice for preventive medication and re-think the dog's day and lifestyle to provide more activity and interest.

What if my dog is weak and lethargic?

97 It is normal and sensible for short-faced dogs, elderly dogs and pregnant bitches to be lethargic in hot weather, but general weakness and lethargy can be associated with many serious illnesses. Thus it is generally wise to seek veterinary attention.

Possible causes which a vet may consider include:

- Obesity – see 'What if?' no.67.
- Diabetes.
- Anaemia.
- Heart disease.
- Lack of thyroid hormone.

Lethargy can signify underlying illness.

What if my dog has collapsed and is comatose?

98 Any disease or condition which makes breathing difficult may cause a dog to collapse temporarily, e.g. heat stroke – see 'What if?' no.76.

Short-nosed dogs (Boxers, Pekingese, Pugs, Bulldogs) taking violent exercise may faint through lack of oxygen. A few minutes rest, plus dousing the head with cold water, will generally restore the dog to normal, but the rest of the walk should be controlled on the lead. It is wise to take the dog to a veterinary surgeon to be checked if the problem arises on more than one occasion.

A condition associated with Cavalier King Charles Spaniels causes them to spin round and collapse momentarily unconscious, usually while walking on the lead. No satisfactory explanation has been found, and the dogs usually recover quickly, but the episode is likely to be repeated.

Other causes of collapse include:

Low blood sugar (hypoglycaemia) The condition may be associated with irregular feeding times, distress, or exhaustion. Immediate action: Feed something sweet at once, an energy bar or the equivalent is ideal, but it *must* be one which does *not* contain chocolate. Subsequently ask for your dog to be checked thoroughly by a veterinary surgeon.

Slipped disc This condition occurs most frequently in short-legged, long-backed breeds. Affected dogs may show intense pain, weakness and unsteadiness on all four limbs or absolute paralysis of the hind limbs. There may also be a loss of bladder control. Keep the dog still, transport the dog without delay to the veterinary surgery carefully to avoid causing it pain. Be prepared for a long recovery process and possibly permanent paralysis (paraplegia).

Dogs suffering from hypothermia will feel cold to the touch. They need to be kept warm and transported promptly to a veterinary surgery.

Hypothermia (following exposure to intense cold) Affected dogs are cold to the touch. Apply gentle warmth, keep the dog loosely covered, until you reach the veterinary surgery. Give the dog a warm drink that it likes and has drunk before if it is able to swallow; do *not* give brandy or other spirits.

Shock (following road accident or haemorrhage) Shocked dogs feel cold to the touch, and appear limp, lifeless, with rapid shallow breathing. Lips and gums and the lining of the eyelids become very pale. *Seek the nearest vet immediately*. An intravenous drip will almost certainly be required. Give nothing by mouth, cover the dog loosely and keep it warm. Collapse may also be associated with:
• Diabetes, particularly following an overdose of insulin.
• Heart disease.
• Kidney disease.
• Poisoning (e.g. through ingesting antifreeze or human medicines).
In all these cases seek veterinary help so that an accurate diagnosis can be made and the appropriate medication given.

What if my dog is not breathing?

99 Lie the animal flat on its side, open its mouth, pull the tongue forward and check that there is nothing obstructing the throat, and that the airway is clear. It may be necessary to apply intermittent pressure on the chest and even try resuscitating the dog by gently blowing up its nose while keeping its mouth closed. See Part 2, 'What if?' no.40.

What if my dog appears deaf?

100

Congenital deafness is often associated with white coat colouring, and is known to occur in Dalmatians, Bull Terriers, white Boxers, Cocker Spaniels and several small terrier breeds. Deafness in puppies does not usually become apparent until about five weeks of age. Deafness may not be recognized in situations where affected puppies can copy the actions of other litter members.

Congenital deafness cannot be treated, and euthanasia is usually advised as acute hearing is of vital importance to a dog for self-preservation, interaction with other dogs, and obedience to its owner's commands.

Elderly dogs often become progressively deaf. By this age, however, they have learned to respond to their owner's wishes and they are not highly active, so deafness is not such a handicap to them provided the owner bears their disability in mind. It is worth asking your veterinary surgeon's advice to check that there is no underlying disease or condition causing the deafness which could be treated, such as the accumulation of wax in the ear canal.

White Boxers may be congenitally deaf.

What if my dog is salivating excessively?

101

It is normal for dogs with loose lower lips to exude more saliva than those with tight mouths. It is also normal for a dog to drool when eagerly awaiting food, and dogs do drool in the presence of an in-season bitch. Fear and anxiety can give rise to drooling and over-production of saliva is a frequent prelude to car sickness. Where none of these explanations applies, excessive and continual salivation should prompt a visit to your veterinary surgeon.

Excessive salivation may be associated with problems in the mouth which may cause difficulty in eating (see 'What if?' no.91) and also as a result of swallowing something poisonous.

What if my dog is over-sexed?
(See also Part 1, 'What if?' no.5)

102

Sex drive in the dog is expressed in mounting behaviour, territory marking, roaming, destructiveness and aggression to other dogs. Males of the small breeds and mongrels up to medium size are more inclined to hypersexual behaviour than males of large and giant breeds.

It is normal for a healthy, young male dog to have a vigorous sex drive, especially if he is kept with or near entire bitches

coming into season (on heat). Many adolescent males go through a short period of hypersexual behaviour at puberty (6-14 months), but in most dogs this behaviour is short-lived. Dogs do not 'need' a bitch at this time and it is far preferable never to use a companion dog at stud.

Castration of Dogs Castration involves removing both testicles through a small incision at the front of the scrotal sac. The scrotum itself is left empty and the fact that the testicles have been removed is not obvious on casual observation. The operation is carried out under general anaesthetic from which dogs usually recover rapidly. The small wound generally heals within four to six days and without complication.

The operation may be carried out to reduce the size of the prostate when that gland is enlarged (prostatic hypertrophy) and when tumours are present in the testes.

Castration does not usually affect the dog's intelligence, playfulness or guarding ability when carried out after puberty. There is, however, a tendency for dogs to put on weight after the operation but this can generally be controlled by reducing the dog's calorie intake and increasing the amount of exercise given.

You do not have to put up with hypersexual traits, like mounting behaviour. A vet will be able to advise on the best course of preventive action.

Castration is often advocated to control hypersexual traits in dogs. The effect of castration on these traits is dependent to some extent on the severity of the signs seen and the length of time they have been a problem. For this reason vets sometimes first test the likely effect of castration by blocking male hormone production with a female hormone.

Many owners have, in the past, regarded these behaviours as being part and parcel of owning a dog, but nowadays it is not necessary to put up with such inconveniences. There is little point in having a dog and suffering with it!

Ask your veterinary surgeon for his advice in respect of this matter. Your vet will be able to advise you on the best course of action, including the possibility of applying the behaviour control methods we have described earlier, either alone or in conjunction with the operation. See also Part 1, 'What if' no.5, page 30.

Feminine Problems

What if my bitch is drinking excessively?

103

Possible Causes and Other Important Signs:
• Pyometra – usually related to a recent heat in middle-aged bitches. In some cases there is an obnoxious bloody vaginal discharge – see page 98.
• Diabetes – see page 95.

Action: This is a serious sign in bitches and unless it is obviously associated with hot weather or excessive exercise, *veterinary help should be sought without delay*. It may be useful to take a urine sample with you when consulting your vet, and be sure that you are able to tell the vet exactly when your bitch was last on heat.

What if my bitch is going bald?

104

Possible Causes and Other Important Signs:
• Sometimes a consequence of spaying.
• Ovarian tumours – often some abdominal distension and a history of not being on heat (anoestrus) for two years or more.

Action: The baldness is usually bilaterally symmetrical where it is associated with abnormal hormone levels. Because successful treatment depends on correct diagnosis, which in turn may have to be supported by the examination of blood samples to determine hormone levels, a veterinary consultation is sensible but is not urgently required.

What if my bitch is passing urine more frequently?

105

Possible Causes and Other Important Signs:
• Inflammation of the vagina (vaginitis) – a vaginal discharge and frequent licking of the vagina.
• Territory marking in association with heat.
• Inflammation of the urinary bladder (cystitis).
• Pyometra – see page 98.
• Diabetes mellitus – see page 95.

Action: Unless obviously associated with territory marking, veterinary attention should be sought within 24 hours so that the cause may be diagnosed and proper treatment instigated. Veterinary attention is certainly needed if the urine contains blood. Take a urine sample.

What if my bitch is incontinent?

Possible Causes and Other Important Signs:

- In relation to spaying particularly before puberty (and in large breeds).
- Over-submissiveness (see Part 1, 'What if?' no.9).
- Inflammation of the urinary bladder (cystitis).

Action: Seek veterinary help. Unless the urine contains blood there is time to try to establish whether the incontinence is linked to some specific factor or event.

What if my bitch is passing blood-stained, smelly urine with difficulty?

107

Possible Causes and Other Important Signs:

- Inflammation of the vagina (vaginitis).
- Inflammation of the urinary bladder (cystitis) and stones in the bladder (urolithiasis).
- Vaginal tumours and swelling of the vaginal mucous membrane (vaginal hyperplasia).

- Possibly inflammation of the womb (metritis) and pyometra – see page 98.
- Bitch on heat.
- Post-whelping.

Action: Obtain veterinary treatment *without delay*, unless the problem is associated with heat or recent whelping. Take a urine sample to the surgery.

Bitches that have recently whelped sometimes pass urine which contains some blood.

What if my bitch is pot-bellied?

108

Possible Causes and Other Important Signs:

- Pregnancy – enlarged mammary glands and possibly the production of some milk.
- False pregnancy – see pages 97-8.
- Inflammation of the urinary bladder (cystitis) with urine retention – abdominal pain and frequent attempts to pass urine.
- Pyometra – see page 98.

Action: As there are numerous causes veterinary attention should be sought. If the abdominal enlargement is gross and has appeared suddenly, or if the bitch is also vomiting or collapsed, *seek help urgently*.

What if my bitch has a lump or swelling?

109

Possible Causes and Other Important Signs:
- Mammary tumours.
- Inflammation of the mammary gland (mastitis).

- Mammary congestion – swollen mammary glands, but not inflamed; usually no rise in body temperature.
- Swelling of the vaginal mucous membrane (vaginal hyperplasia).
- Vaginal polyps – possibly straining to pass blood-stained urine.
- Vaginal prolapse – an obvious swelling protruding from the vagina and straining to pass urine.

Action: Except in the case of suspected mastitis or a vaginal prolapse that has become traumatised, veterinary help is not required urgently. However it is better to ask for assistance earlier rather than later so that effective treatment can be started promptly.

Swelling of the mammary glands or the presence of lumps is not uncommon – see also page 99. Expert advice will be needed to determine the cause.

What if my bitch is licking her vulva excessively?

110

Possible Causes and Other Important Signs:
- In association with coming on heat or whelping – see pages 144-5.
- Inflammation of the urinary bladder (cystitis).
- Swelling of the vaginal mucous membrane (vaginal hyperplasia).
- Vaginal polyps and inflammation of the vagina (vaginitis).
- Pyometra – see page 98.
- Inflammation of the womb (metritis).

Action: Since the causes are legion, diagnosis by a veterinary surgeon is required. The urgency of the situation will be determined by the bitch's general appearance and/or the presence of other more worrying signs such as persistent vomiting or continual straining to pass urine.

What if my bitch has a vaginal discharge?

111

Possible Causes and Other Important Signs:
- Open pyometra – see page 98.
- Inflammation of the womb (metritis).
- Inflammation of the urinary bladder (cystitis).
- In association with heat or post-whelping.
- Inflammation of the vagina (vaginitis).

Action: *Seek veterinary attention without delay* especially if the bitch is also vomiting, is obviously 'off colour' and has recently been on heat, since emergency surgery may be needed. Cases of suspected metritis in newly-whelped bitches also need prompt medical attention.

What if my bitch is mated by accident?

112

Action: If it is known that a bitch has been accidentally mated, veterinary help should be sought without delay. Action needs to be taken promptly, as an oestrogen injection, or the start of a course of injections, must be given within three to seven days of the mating to avert pregnancy. These injections, which are unfortunately not always effective and may be associated with adverse side effects, will often cause the bitch to begin her heat all over again and she may be even more willing to be mated on the second occasion. Adequate control measures to ensure that the bitch is not mated again will be particularly important in that situation.

Recently a product containing a compound which acts as a progesterone antagonist has been introduced. Two injections are needed 24 hours apart and they can be given much later in pregnancy – from 0-45 days after mating. However early administration is more effective. Your veterinary surgeon will advise what course of action is most appropriate in any particular case. The options will be greater if you seek help early.

In cases of suspected mismating, owners should be prepared to provide their veterinary surgeon with a full history of the event. Sometimes swabs are taken from the vagina to establish whether or not a mating has taken place.

It is dangerous to the bitch's health to rely continually on averting pregnancy after mismating; adequate **preventive** measures must be considered. In the case of bitches not intended for breeding, spaying is generally the action of choice. Vets will sometimes advise that bitches are spayed about three to four weeks after the mismating rather than giving misalliance hormone injections and then spaying the bitch later.

Injections can be given to avert pregnancy if a bitch is mated by accident while on heat. However, unless you particularly want to breed from your bitch, it makes more sense to spay female dogs. Spaying involves the surgical removal of the womb and ovaries.

What if my bitch is found to be pregnant unexpectedly?

113 Consult your veterinary surgeon as soon as is convenient. If pregnancy is not too far advanced and you are anxious not to have a litter of puppies, it may be possible to spay the bitch, removing the uterus with the foetuses inside at the same time.

What if my bitch has signs of abdominal pain?

114 Some bitches may show signs of abdominal pain and lack of appetite when they are about to come on heat. Heat in bitches is comprised of two stages, each lasting nine days on average. The first, pro-oestrus, is marked by the blood-stained discharge; the second, oestrus, is the time when the bitch will accept the male. If the pain is persistent and severe, seek veterinary help since there may be some other underlying cause of the pain.

What if my bitch is a problem when on heat?

115 The main reasons why bitch owners should control heat in their pets if they do not wish to breed at all are:

- To gain a health advantage: the risk of the bitch developing uterine problems, particularly pyometra, and suffering from false pregnancy or swelling of the vaginal mucous membrane (vaginal hyperplasia) is eliminated and the incidence of mammary tumours is much reduced.
- To prevent unwanted pregnancy and indiscriminate breeding.
- To make the pet more consistently companionable: a bitch's temperament changes during heat and during the subsequent month or so, especially if she suffers from false pregnancy.
- To make owning a bitch more convenient; to avoid problems of messy bleeding, unsightly vulval swelling, attractiveness to dogs and the need to keep the bitch confined – or at least under very close observation – for three weeks, twice a year. Spayed bitches will be less inclined to stray.

AAWHHOOOOO!!

Heat can be controlled by spaying or chemically by using an artificial hormone similar to that contained in the human 'pill'. Each method has advantages and disadvantages and the matter should be discussed in depth with a veterinary surgeon so that the most appropriate action can be chosen to suit your particular pet and circumstances. It is important to realize that the choice will be different for different breeds and will vary according to the owner's needs. Some bitches, especially in the small breeds, spay well with a low risk of side effects, but in large breeds the possibility of subsequent urinary incontinence cannot be ignored. Spayed bitches may be more inclined to put on weight. However, this tendency is usually quite easily controlled by decreasing the bitch's calorie intake and increasing the amount of exercise taken. Regular weighing of spayed bitches is a sensible precaution. In some breeds a coat change may occur after the operation. Spaniels, Retrievers and Collies may develop a more woolly coat and short-haired breeds like Dobermanns may develop bald patches on their flanks.

If you wish to obtain the benefits noted above, discuss the subject with your veterinary surgeon **before** your bitch's first season, at around five months of age. Bitches are usually spayed, provided they are healthy, at any time **after** their first season, but **not** while on heat or if they are showing signs of false pregnancy. Some vets advocate spaying before the first heat, but most consider that it is generally better to let bitches experience the hormonal changes associated with at least one heat so that they become properly mature physically and mentally.

One of the disadvantages of owning a bitch on heat is the unwanted attention she will attract from many of the male dogs in the vicinity.

Puppies look sweet but they require a major time commitment from an owner. Spaying confers health benefits on the bitch and removes any chance that you will have to cope with an unexpected litter.

145

Do remember that dogs need mental stimulation to keep them alert and happy as well as physical exercise.

PREVENTION OF ILLNESS

Health checks

Make grooming your dog a regular part of your daily routine. Make it easy for yourself by setting aside a place for this activity and install a bench or shelf at an appropriate height if your dog is not too heavy to lift. Use good grooming tools – a metal comb that has rounded teeth set into the spine and a good quality

TIPS ON KEEPING YOUR DOG FIT AND WELL – DO'S AND DON'T'S

DO –

- Register your dog with a veterinary surgeon.
- Make sure your dog is fully protected by vaccination.
- Carry out health checks yourself regularly. Work to a regular pattern starting with your dog's head and moving down the body systematically.
- Feed a balanced diet.
- Groom your dog daily and have it clipped or trimmed regularly if it belongs to a breed where that is necessary.
- Arrange to have your dog's nails clipped if you notice them getting too long.
- Exercise your dog regularly both on and off the lead.
- Weigh your dog at least two to three times a year to ensure that it is not becoming overweight (see 'What if?' no.67).

- Bath your dog as necessary but at least twice a year. Encourage swimming – it is good exercise and good for your dog's coat and its safety.
- Ensure that your dog has a good bed and bedding materials that can be easily washed and disinfected. The use of Vet Bed is recommended by most vets and strong plastic beds are to be preferred to wicker-work baskets.
- Keep records of your dog's illnesses and any treatments given.
- Worm your dog regularly – your vet will advise.
- Insure your dog fully to cover the cost of unexpected veterinary medication and possibly third-party claims.
- Make sure that your dog is properly identified with an up-to-date, easily readable identity disc and a modern microchip or a tattoo.

Regular clipping prevents nails from getting too long. If your dog's paws click as it walks on hard flooring, they probably need clipping.

brush. If you want advice, ask at your veterinary practice, a good petshop or grooming parlour, or the breeder if you have a pedigree dog.

Carrying out a number of routine daily and weekly checks on all dogs when they are groomed makes a lot of sense. Your dog needs and will appreciate the attention. Properly done, such checks and observations enable you to spot the signs of illness early and seek veterinary attention promptly or more leisurely as appropriate.

Consider having your dog checked on a yearly basis by your veterinary surgeon – an annual MOT is no bad thing.

can be distracted by a cat running loose.

- Consider having your bitch spayed. That can provide definite health advantages (see 'What if?' no.115).
- Obtain good quality eating and drinking bowls that can be easily cleaned daily and regularly disinfected. Stainless steel or pottery bowls are generally better than plastic bowls.

DON'T –

- Play overly energetic games and avoid playing tug-of-war games especially if your dog belongs to one of the breeds bred for guarding.
- Be tempted to gain favours by giving titbits that have not been earned.
- Forget to exercise your dog's mind as well as its body.
- Let your dog off the lead near main roads – even the best-trained dogs

- Give your dog bones and certainly not chicken bones that can splinter or other bones that can be chewed into a powder.
- Delay consulting your vet if you are at all worried.
- Throw pebbles on the beach or any other hard objects for your dog to catch.
- Leave your dog in your car in the sun – *ever*.
- Under any circumstances let your dog roam.
- Let your dog travel with its head outside the car window.
- Give your dog human chocolate. Dark chocolate is especially toxic to dogs. Garden coconut shell mulch can be equally dangerous.
- Let your dog have access to cupboards or garages where cleaning fluids, garden sprays and the like are kept.

THE AGEING DOG – MAINTAINING QUALITY OF LIFE IN OLD AGE

PART 4

CONTENTS

- **INTRODUCTION** Page 150
- **TIPS TO IMPROVE YOUR DOG'S QUALITY OF LIFE – DO'S AND DON'T'S** Page 150

WHAT IFs...?

What if my dog...

116 should become senile? Page 151

117 is becoming deaf? Page 151

118 is losing its sight? Page 151

119 is becoming incontinent? Page 152

120 has digestive problems? Page 152

121 appears to be suffering from arthritis? Page 152

122 becomes very ill and has a reduced quality of life? Should I consider having it put to sleep (euthanasia)? Page 153

- **GRIEVING** Page 153
- **OBTAINING ANOTHER DOG** Page 153

Remember that advancing years do not have to mean a declining quality of life. The loving partnership that you have formed with your dog will help to ensure that it continues to enjoy life to the full into old age. Regular health checks are particularly important so that any problems are spotted early and the appropriate actions are taken promptly.

INTRODUCTION

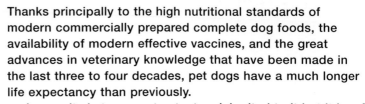

Thanks principally to the high nutritional standards of modern commercially prepared complete dog foods, the availability of modern effective vaccines, and the great advances in veterinary knowledge that have been made in the last three to four decades, pet dogs have a much longer life expectancy than previously.

Longevity is to a great extent an inherited trait but it is, of course, also dependent on good care by the owner. The life expectancy of smaller breeds is of the order of 14 years and even 17 years is not uncommon. However, giant breeds, and Bulldogs especially, seldom live longer than 8-10 years of age. Greying of the muzzle and eyebrows is seen in some dogs as early as 5 years old but that does not mean that they should be treated as old age pensioners or provided with a zimmer frame! In extreme old age the whole coat may become dusted with white hairs and some dogs go grey or even white all over.

TIPS TO IMPROVE YOUR DOG'S QUALITY OF LIFE

DO –

- Monitor the amount of water that your dog drinks daily. Increased thirst is often a significant sign in older dogs and can be associated with failing kidneys or diabetes, for example.
- Feed your dog food that it really enjoys. Warming the meal will make it more appetizing. Consider providing a bowl that is more 'user friendly' and placing it at a more convenient height.
- Carry out health checks regularly so that any pending disease or condition is noted early. Prompt medication is especially important in older dogs.

DON'T –

- Turn your dog out on cold winter mornings. The shock of very cold air could precipitate a stroke.
- Board your pet unless it is really

necessary. The stress involved, particularly if you use an unfamiliar kennel, could precipitate a latent illness.
- Overfeed your dog; it will need much less food if it is only able to amble a short distance rather than running amok with another dog, joining you on a good hike, or clambering up the nearest mountain. Remember too that obese dogs are more prone to heart disease, arthritis and diabetes (see Part 3, 'What if?' no.67.)
- Over-exercise your dog if it has heart disease, is prone to fits of coughing, has breathing problems, or suffers from painful arthritis.
- Let your ageing dog out on its own; it may well become disorientated, as a result of deteriorating sight and hearing, and be unable to find its way home.

What if my dog should become senile?

116 Senile dogs will show an increased need for their owner's company. They may become disorientated and restless and have good and bad days. If you are worried, ask your vet to give your dog a thorough physical check; some medication may be of help and even prompt recovery. Above all, lots of sympathy and tolerance will go a long way towards making your dog's life much happier.

What if my dog is becoming deaf?

117 See Part 3, 'What if?' no.100. Test your dog's ability to hear regularly using sound at differing volumes and pitch. Make allowances for any hearing impairment and keep your dog close to you on walks and protect it from danger. Use gestures to communicate with your dog (see Part 1). A veterinary check at six-monthly or yearly intervals is a good idea.

What if my dog is losing its sight?

118 See Part 3, 'What if?' no.73. Book your dog in for a veterinary check to see if there is any treatment that could improve the situation. Keep the dog's surroundings unchanged as far as possible; don't move furniture etc. simply for aesthetic reasons.

Ageing dogs with impaired vision can still enjoy a good quality of life if their owners treat them with patience, love and tolerance.

What if my dog is becoming incontinent?

119 See Part 3, 'What if?' no.85. Although such 'leaks' may simply be due to a reluctance or possibly reduced ability to get out of its bed, it is sensible to have your dog checked for any underlying condition which may be to blame. Specific medication can help in many cases. Needless to say you must be considerate and avoid chastising your dog if it should have an accident. Simply resolve to take it out to be clean at more frequent intervals.

If your dog's stomach becomes rather delicate as it grows into old age, consider gradually changing its diet to a formulation that is more easily digested.

What if my dog has digestive problems?

120 See Part 3, 'What if?' nos.79, 81-83. Consider reverting to a puppy-feeding regime with three or four smaller meals daily. Special commercially prepared diets which have increased palatability and which are more easily digested are now available from veterinary surgeons in a number of different flavours. Be prepared to ask for advice from your vet or the practice nurse.

What if my dog appears to be suffering from arthritis?

121 See Part 3, 'What if?' no.89. Don't despair because arthritis is common in ageing dogs. The condition has been researched thoroughly and many very effective products are now available. Your veterinary surgeon will recommend the medication that is most suitable for your needs and will work out a cost-effective dosage regime.

What if my dog becomes very ill and has a reduced quality of life? Should I consider having it put to sleep (euthanasia)?

Saying goodbye to a much-loved family pet is a very hard thing to do. But make the dog's quality of life your prime consideration – it's not kind to let it linger on in pain and distress simply because you cannot face taking the ultimate decision.

122 Many people consider dogs to be lucky in that euthanasia is an option for them. A dog can slip away with quiet dignity following a simple injection into a vein in its foreleg. Do be guided by your vet; he or she will tell you when the time for this action is near.

Be ruled entirely by consideration for your dog and do what you feel in your heart to be best for it. Too many owners are reluctant to make this decision, perhaps because they don't want to cut short what has been an enjoyable and fruitful companionship. That is understandable, but a decision to have a dog put to sleep must never stem from self-interest to satisfy your own need or desire.

Don't be tempted to say 'let's give it another week or two'. Weeks can soon become months or even years with your dog becoming more and more unwell and possibly enduring increasing pain. It is far better to set a definite time limit, saying, together with your vet, that if your dog can't do this or that any more, or degenerates in any definitive way, or its quality of life has declined significantly, then you will opt for euthanasia without more delay.

Making a thoroughly discussed and timely decision to have your dog 'put to sleep' means that you will have fond memories of your dog and recall the good days when it was healthy and full of life, rather than remembering it as a chronically suffering invalid with a poor quality of life.

Grieving

Finally, whether your dog dies naturally or is put to sleep, do be prepared to accept its death as a natural conclusion to its life.

Give yourself permission to grieve and face the pain as it occurs. Allow yourself all the time or space you need to accept your loss – crying, talking to others and writing things down are all acceptable ways of releasing your emotion. If you have children, talk to them in simple but truthful terms about what has happened to your pet and what plans you have made for burial, cremation or other means of disposing of your pet's body. Children need to know that in death their pet has been treated with respect.

Obtaining Another Dog

Do take time to consider whether or not to have another pet. Don't think or talk in terms of replacement – that's not giving a new pet a fair chance. All dogs are different, they must certainly not be treated as clones. A new dog will, of course, have its own personality, but it will also be largely what *you* make it. It's up to you to give it the best possible chance to grow into an ideal dog.

INDEX

Note: Page numbers set in *italic type* refer to picture captions; page numbers set in **bold type** refer to the subject of a 'What if…' entry.

A

abdominal diseases 127
abdominal pain in bitches **144**
abscesses 133, 135
accidents 86-7 *see also* wounds
  artificial respiration for dog 69, *69*
  barbed wire, thorns **82**
  burns or scalds **66**, **134**
  chest injuries 116
  drowning 115-16, *115*
  electric shock **69**, *69*, 86
  human medication ingested **68**
  insect bites and stings **83**, 95, *95*, 111, 133, *133*, 136
  poisonous plants 86, 122-3, 137-8
  poisonous substances 103, 122-3, 125, 137-8, 147
  road traffic **81**, *81*, 109, 116, 125, 129, 137
  swallowed foreign body 115
adopted dogs *see* rescue dogs
aggression 24, 27-8, **30**, **33**, *33*, 35, 67, *67*, 82, 138 *see also* fighting
  and castration 33, 139
  towards children 30, 34, 67
  towards other dogs 31, **33**, *33*, 67, *67*, 138
  towards people 30
airway obstruction 114-16 *see also* drowning
allergies in dogs 94-5, 111-2, 116-7, 133
allergies in owner 57
anaemia 136
anal adenomata 121
anal furunculosis 121
anal gland problems 121, *121*
anaphylaxis 95
animal behaviourists 12, 27-8, 37, 44-5, 49, 56
antibiotics 82
anti-chew sprays 62
antiseptics 66, 82, 134

anxiety 24, 34, *34*, 45 *see also* separation anxiety
anxiolytic drugs 45
arthritis 42, 63, 105, 124, 128,
  in older dogs 150, 152
ascites (accumulation of fluid in abdominal cavity) 127, *127*
association, training by 16, 18-21, *18-19*
  classical conditioning 18, 20-1
  during walks 19
  harmonization of commands 19
  instrumental conditioning 18, *18*
  timing of commands 19
  timing of training 19
asthma 95

B

babies, dogs and **60**, *60*, 86
bacterial infections 122
bad breath **130-1**, *131* *see also* teeth
balanitis (inflammation of penile sheath) 126
balanoposthitis (inflammation of penis and sheath) 126
baldness in bitches **140**
barking, excessive 25, 28, **29**, 48
basic training exercises 20-1, 26, 29, 33, 35, 42, 46
  classes 20
  duration of 20
  when to begin 20
bathing a dog 58, *58*, 146
beach, dogs on **82**, *82*, 147
bed and bedding, dog's 36, *36*, 44, 48, *49*, 55, 59, 61, 83, 117, 124, 146
bed, owner's 56, *56*
Bedlington Terriers 116
begging for food or attention **38**, *38*, 105-6
behavioural problems, analysing 28
behaviour modification techniques 43, 45, 56
  systematic desensitization 45
  using CD 45
Belgian Shepherd Dogs 121
bitches 42, 52-3, 56, **71-2**, *71*, 76,

78, **84-5**, *85*, 91, 95, 97-9, *97*, 99, *99*, 100-1, 103-4, 108, 114, 116, *122*, 124-5, *124*, 126, 136, 138-9
  specific health problems of 140-5
biting, nipping, snapping **29**, 48, 63 *see also* puppies
biting tail **121**
bladder stones 96, *96*, 124-5, *125*
bleach 55-6
blindness or impaired vision *see* eyes
bloat *see* gastric dilation and torsion
blood-filled swelling *see* haematoma
blood in faeces **123**
blood in urine **125**
blood staining 52-3, **72**
body language of dogs 13-15, *14-15*, 43, *43*
  ears 14, *15*, *43*
  eyes 14, *15*
  mouth 14
  shaking 43, *43*
  tail *14-15*, 15
body language of humans 13, *13*, 14, 19, 24, 35, 56, 151
bone fractures 128
bones (feeding) 147
bowel problems 122-3
Boxers *22*, 114, 136, 138, *138*
brain problems 114, 132
breaking wind **120-1** *see also* flatulence
breath *see* bad breath
breathing, abnormal **114-16**, 150
  failure to breathe **137**
  panting *114*
breed rescue societies 78
bronchitis 129
Bulldogs 136, 150
Bull Terriers 57, 138
burns and scalds *see* accidents

C

calculus *see* teeth
cancer 108
canine adeno virus 94
canine coronovirus 94
canine distemper 93, 129, 132
canine enteritis 94

canine herpes virus 94

canine insurance 77, 79, 91, 146

canine parainfluenza virus 94

canine parvovirus 94, 103, 123

canine shampoo 54, 58 see also bathing

car, dog and 34, 48, 54, **57**, 87, 109, 123

dog guard 87

hair shedding in **57**

heat stroke danger **84**, 114-15, 147

with baby 60

with children in car 34, 48

car sickness **34**, *34*, 103, 138

carbon tetrachloride 54

castration (chemical and surgical) 30, 33, 71, 74, 80, 96, 139 see also neutering; spaying

cats and kittens **61**, *61*, 133, 135

Cavalier King Charles Spaniels 136

chase behaviour **32**, *32*

and animals 32

and cyclists 32, *32*

and people 32

chewing family possessions **29**

chewing furnishings **62**

chew objects 49, 62, 72, 83, 86

Chihuahuas 80

chocolate, dangers of 65, **68**, *68*, 86, 147 see also doggy choc drops

choke chains 73

Christmas see festivities

citronella 56

clicker training 24-5

Cocker Spaniels 138

cocoa powder/mulch see chocolate

collar and lead, use of 20, *20*, 44, 48, 58, **73**, *73*, 80-1, 87, 146-7 see also pulling on lead

Collies 110, 145

colon tumours 122

coma **136-7**, *137*

'Come' command and gesture 18, 20, *21*, 32-3, 35

compact discs (CD) in habituation/socialization training 17

conditioning (Pavlov) 20-1

congestive heart failure 95

constipation 65, 96, 100, 120, **123**, *123*, 131

convulsions see fits

coprophagia (eating faeces) **34-5**

Corgis 29

coughing, persistent **129**, *129*, 150

crates see dog crates

cryotherapy 133

cryptorchidism 96-7

cuts see wounds

cystitis 42, 124-5, 140-3

D

Dachshunds 68, 76

Dalmatians *96*, 138

deafness **138**, *138*

in older dogs **150**

defecation on command 21

dermatitis 117

destructive behaviour 25, 30, 35, 43, 138

detergents, uses of 54, 66

deterrent sprays 25, *25*, 56, 62

diabetes 42, 95, 105, 108, 136-7, 140, 150

diarrhoea 82, 90, 95, 100, 103, 121, **122**, *122*

diet see feeding

digestive tract problems 65, *65* see also feeding

digging in garden **76**, *76*

discharge from penis **126**

discharge from vulva **126**

disinfectants 52-3, 55

dislocated joints 128

disobedience when called **33**, 48

distemper see canine distemper

Dobermanns 57, 73, 145

Dog-appeasing Pheromone (DAP) 25, 44

dog basket see bed

dog bed see bed

dog behaviourist see animal behaviourist

dog breeders 49, 58, 63, 71, 110, 147

dog crates 36, 40, 47, *47*, 55, *55*, 59, 62, 87

doggy choc drops 68

dog pox 142

dominant behaviour 25-6, *27*, 28, 31, **35**, 39, 56, 63, 79 see also leadership/dominance exercises

'Down' (lie down) command and gesture 18-20, *21*, 29, 31

drinking, excessive **108**, *108*, 125

in bitches **140**

in older dogs 150

drowning 115-16, *115*

E

ears 42, 63, 114 see also deafness

bacterial infections 112-3

cleaning 113, *113*

ear canker (otitis externa) 112-4, *114*

ear mites 112

excess hair in 113, *113*

foreign bodies in 112

fungus or yeast infection 112

inflammation of inner ear (otis interna) 114

oral haematoma 114

shaking or scratching **112-3**, *112-3*

swelling on ear flap 133

wax in ear canal 138

eating faeces see coprophagia

eating with difficulty *see* feeding
eclampsia (lactation tetany) 97, 114, 132
electric shock *see* accidents
electronic identity chip (microchip) 78, *78*, 146
Elizabethan collar 134
emaciation (excessive thinness) **108**
enlarged prostate (prostatic hypertrophy) 139
enzyme deficiencies 122
epilepsy 95-6, *95*, 132
euthanasia 30, 36, **153**, *153*
  grieving 153
  obtaining another dog 153
exercise 30, 39, 48, 54, 60, 104, 108, *108*, 114, 123, 139, 145-7, *146*
  mental stimulation 146-7, *146*

excessive dominance *see* dominant behaviour
excitability 30
extending lead 33
external parasite infections 101, 117
  see also fleas

extinction *see* punishment, by ignoring
eyes
  abnormal appearance **110-11**
  anatomical defects 110
  blindness **112**
  blue eye 93, 111
  'cherry eye' (enlarged Harderian gland) 111
  cataract 110-11
  collie eye anomaly (CEA) 110
  conjunctivitis 110
  glaucoma *110*, 111
  impaired vision in older dogs **151**, *151*
  keratitis (corneal ulcer) 111
  lens luxation 110
  progressive retinal atrophy (PRA) 110-11
  ptosis 111
  runny eyes **109-10**, *110*

F

face/head collar 20, 37, 73, *73*
facial abscess 131
facial expressions of dogs *see* body language of dogs
faeces 122-3
  blood in **123**
  dog WC 76
  disposal of **76-7**, 101
  eating *see* coprophagia
  passing in garden **76-7**, *76*
  passing on pavement **74**, *74*
failure to pass urine **124**
false pregnancy 97-8, *97*, 99, 101, 127, 141, 144-5
family, dog's place in *12*, 27, *27*, 46, *46*, 67
fearfulness 30, 43, 45
feeding 39, 48, 55, 57, 59-60, **70-1**, *70-1*, 73, 87, 103, 108, 116, 120-3, 126-7, *127*, 130-1, 139, 145-7 *see also* teeth
  changes in feeding **70-1**, 120, 122
  commercial dog foods 70-1, *70-1*, 104-6, 150, 152
  cow's milk 71
  complementary diets 70, 106

eating with difficulty **130**, *130*
  home-made diets 70-1, 104, 120
  older dogs 150, **152**, *152*
  refusal to eat **104**
  slimming tips 105
fences, importance of 30
festivities, dogs and **65**, *65*
fighting 67, *67*, **79-80**, *79-80*, 114, 116
  with cat 133, 135
fireworks *see* phobias
first-aid after accident 81, *81*, 83, 116, 134-5, *134*
first-aid kit 87
Fitness Assessment Score Card 106-7
fitness do's and don't's 146-7
fits **132** *see also* epilepsy; rabies
flatulence 105, 120-1
fleas, lice, ticks and mites 58, 61, 100-1, 112, 117-9, *118-9*
  cheyletiella (rabbit fur mite) 117, *117*
  demodectic mange 117
  flea sprays *118*, 119
  insecticidal collars 119
  insecticides 119
  Ixodes ricinus tick *117*
  nits 119
  oral medications 119
  Sarcoptes mite *101*
  Sarcoptic mange mite 117
  Trichodectes canis lice 119, *119*
food rewards *see* rewarding good behaviour
foreign body lodged in mouth 130, *130*

G

games 35, 48, *49*, 147
  tug of war 35, 48, 147
gastric dilation and torsion (bloat) 114, 127, *127* *see also* pot belly
genitals, excessive licking of **126**
German Shepherd Dogs 116, *116*, 121
gingivitis (inflammation of gums) 131
grass, eating **102**
grazes *see* wounds

grooming 42, *42*, 57, *57*, **63**, *63*, 146-7
guard dogs 104, 147
gum disease 130-1 *see also* gingivitis; teeth

H

habituation/socialization training 16-17, *16-17*, 43, 46. 48
  for puppies 16-17, *16*, 22, 47, *47*
  using compact discs (CD) 17
  with other animals 16-17, *16-17*
  with people 16-17
haematoma 133
haematuria *see* blood in urine
haemorrhage 137
hair shedding **116**, *116*
  in car **57**
  in house **57**
harnesses, use of 20, 73, 87
head collar *see* face/head collar
head held to one side **114** *see also* ears
health checks and records 91, 146, 150
heart problems 94-5, 105, 127, 129, 131, 136-7, 150
heat (season) in bitches 42, 56, **71-2**, *71*, 78, **84-5**, 91, 98-9, 101, 104, 124-6, 138-43, **144-5**, *145*
  chemical control of 145
heat intolerance and heat stroke **84**, 105, 114-15, 136
'Heel' training and command 18, 20, *20*, 37, 73, *73*
  using collar and lead 20, *20*
  using harness 20
Helpline 77
hierarchy *see* family, dog's place in; leadership/dominance exercises
hormonal problems 57, 108, 116, 127, 136, 140
'house rules' 48, 56-7, *56*, 86
house soiling *see* soiling
house-training 21, **40-2**, *40-1*, 47, **55**, 124
  adult dogs **42**, 55, 124
  puppies **40-1**, 47, 55, 124

hydrocephalus *see* water on the brain
hypersexual behaviour 12, **30**, *30*, 42, **138-9**, *139*
hypoglycaemia *see* low blood sugar
hypothermia 137, *137*

I

identity disc 146
illnesses 42, *42*, 52-3, 55, 63, *63*, 65, *65*, 68, 82, 90-147 *see also individual entries*; accidents; bitches
inappropriate behaviour, prevention of 46-9
inappropriate mounting 30, *30*, 138, *139*
incontinence 92, **124-5**, *124-5*
  in bitches **141**
  in older dogs **152**
infectious canine hepatitis 93, 111
injuries *see* accidents; wounds
insect bites *see* accidents
instrumental conditioning *see* association training
internal parasite infections 100-1, 108 *see also* worms and worming
internet *71*
itchy wheals on skin *see* urticaria

J

jealousy **31**, 56, 60
  of new baby 60
  of other dog 31, 67, *67*
jumping up 25, **31**, 48, 60

K

kennel cough 94, 129
kennels 92, 104, 150
  misbehaviour in **83**, *83*
kidney problems 42, 103, 108, 125, 131, 137, 150

L

Labradors 39, 116, 122
lactation 108,116
language of dogs 13, *13 see also* body language of dogs
laryngitis 129
lawn, bleaching by urination **84**

lead *see* collar and lead
leadership/dominance exercises 26-27, *27*, 29-35, 39, 42, 46, 48, 63, 72, 79
learning process of dogs 16-19, *16-19*
'Leave' command 18, 33, 35, 79
leptospirosis 94, 125
lethargy *see* weakness and lethargy
lice *see* fleas etc.
licking, excessive 25, **38**, 60 *see also* puppies
lick granuloma 136
  of areas of body **136**
  of genitals **126**
  of vagina 140
  of vulva **142**
  of wounds 134
life expectancy 150
limping **128-9**, *128-9*
liquid paraffin 123, *123*
liver disease 96, 105, 108, 131-2
loneliness **66-7**
lost dogs **78-9**
low blood sugar (hypoglycaemia) 137
lump or swelling **133**, *133*

M

'magic punishment' and 'set-up' *see* punishment
mammary tumours 99, 133, 142, *142*, 144
mange *see* fleas etc.
mastitis 99, *99*, 142
mating and mismating 71, **84-5**, *85*, **143**, *143*
medication, human *see* accidents
metritis (inflammation of womb) 141-3
microchip *see* electronic identity chip
mongrels 138
moulting *see* hair shedding
mounting *see* bitches; hypersexual behaviour
muscle strains 128

N

nail clipping 146, *147*
name tags and holders 78-9, *79*

naming dogs 48
neoplasia (growths and tumours in mouth) 130
neutering 56
'No' command 18, 24-5, 29, 30, 32-3, 35, 39, 56, 72, 75, 82

O

obedience training 32
  duration of 32
obesity **104-7**, *105*, 136, 146, 150
  see also feeding
odour-eliminating products 41, 52-3, 55-6
'Okay' command 18
older dogs, problems of 12, 20, 120, 123-4, 131, 136, 138, 148-53
orchitis 97
ovarian tumours 140
over-guarding behaviour 30
over-sexed behaviour *see* hypersexual behaviour

P

pack behaviour 67
pancreatic deficiency 121-2
paralysis (paraplegia) 125, 137
parasite infections 122
parties *see* festivities
passing blood in faeces **123**
Pavlov, Ivan 20-1
paws, foreign bodies in 128, *128*
'pecking order' *see* family, dog's place in; pack behaviour
Pekingese 114, 136
penis, discharge from **126**
periodontal disease (accumulation of tartar deposits on teeth) 131

petting and stroking *see* rewarding good behaviour
pharyngitis 129
pheromone therapy *see* Dog-appeasing Pheromone (DAP)
phobias **43-5**, *43-5*, 65
  destructive behaviour and 43
  fireworks 43, *43-4*, 45
  flashing lights 43-4, 65
  loneliness 43
  loud noises 43-4, 65
  other animals 43
  people 43
  puppies and 22
  thunderstorms 43, *44*
  use of CDs and 45, *45*
  use of TV or radio and *44*
pills *see* tablets
playpens 40, 47, 59
pneumonia 94
poisons *see* accidents
police 77, 78
polyps in rectum 123
Poodles 116
'poop scoops' 74, *74*
possessive behaviour over food **39**
postures of dogs *see also* body language of dogs
  aggressive 14-15, *15*
  fearful 14-15, *15*
  normal 14-15, *15*
  playful *14*
  submissive 14-15, *15*; *see also* submissive behaviour, excessive
pot belly 103, **126-7**, *126-7*
  in bitches 141
praise *see* rewarding good behaviour
pregnancy 71, 97, 100-1, 104, 127, 136, 141, 143
  unexpected **144**
  prostatic disease 124-5
  prostatic hyperplasia (enlargement of prostate gland) 96, 123
  prostatic hypertrophy 139
pruritus *see* scratching, excessive
Pugs 136
pulling on lead **37**, 73, *73*

punishment 18, 22-5, 28-9, 35, 38-9, 47, 61, 63, 72, 80
  appropriateness of 24
  by ignoring or banishment (extinction) 23, 27, 29, 31, 38
  'magic punishment' and 'set-up' 23, 29, 31, 34, 39, 56, 62, *62*, 75-6
  painful stimuli 23
  rules for 24
  timing of 18, 23
  using training discs 23, 31, 34
  using water pistol 23, 31-2, *32*
  when to forgo 24, 39, 41, 48, 56, 152
puppies 16-17, *16*, *18*, 19, 22, 26, **29**, 36, **40-2**, 47-8, *47*, 59, *59*, **62-3**, **72-3**, 75, 77, 83, 94, 97-8, 103-4, 122, *122*, 126, 132, 138, 144, *145*
  aggression and 22
  biting hands **72**
  avoidance behaviour 22
  chewing 25, **29**, **62**
  collar and lead, objecting to **73**
  cow's milk and 71
  deafness in 138
  development, stages of 22
  diarrhoea in 122, *122*
  disposal of faeces 77, 101
  dog crates, use of 47, *47*
  exercise 101
  extroverted 26
  grooming **63**
  habituation/socialization periods 22, *22*, 59
  house-training 21-2, **40-2**, *40-1*, 47, 124
  incontinence in 124-5
  introverted 26
  kennels and 83
  licking **72**, *72*
  over-attachment to owner 22
  phobias 22
  punishment 22, 24-5
  puppy playpen 59
  separation anxiety 22
  tablets, administering 64
  teething 114

twitching 132
vaccination 59
worms and worming 100-1
'putting down' see euthanasia
pyometra 98-9, 103, 108, 126-7,
    140, 141, 142, 143, 144

R

rabies 93, 132
raw-hide chews 29, 131
rectum, stricture of 123
re-homing 30
reinforcing learned behaviour 26
rescue dogs and kennels 12, 18, 28,
    36, 77-8
respiratory disease 129
Retrievers 145
rewarding good behaviour 18-19, *18-
    19*, 22-3, *23*, 26-31, 33, 36, 38,
    41-6, 60-1, 63, 73, 79-80, 82, 147
    timing of 18-19, *18-19, 23*
road accidents see accidents
roaming 30, 138, 147
rubbing bottom on ground **121**
runny eyes see eyes

S

safety tips 86-7
salivation, excessive 52-3, **138**
sand, swallowing **82**
scaling see teeth
scavenging for food *103*, 105-6, 120,
    130
scooting bottom on ground *121, 121*
scratching, excessive **117-19**
season see heat in bitches
sea water, drinking 82, 108
senility **151**
separation anxiety 29, **36-7**, *36-7*
    and destructive behaviour 36-7, *37*
septicaemia 125
sexually motivated behaviour 28
shock 96, 137
shyness with people **38**, *38*
signs of illness 90-1
'Sit' command and gesture 18, 18,
    20, *21*, 29-31, 33, 35, 38, 79, 82
skin disease 57

skin parasites *58 see also* fleas
slipped disc 137
sneezing **109**, *109*
socialization 12, *12*, **59-61** *see also*
    habituation/socialization
    with a new baby 60, *60*
    with a new kitten 61, *61*
    with a new puppy 59
    with a resident adult cat 61
soiling in the house 25, **52-7**
    carpets and upholstery **52-3**
    faeces 52-3
    grass stains 52
    hair shedding **57**
    oil 52, **54**, *54*
    saliva (drooling) 52-3
    tar 52, **54**, *54*
    urine 52-3, 55, *55 see also* territorial
    marking
    vomit 52-3
Spaniels 145
spaying 53, 71-2, 95, 98, 116, 124,
    140-1, 143-5, *145*, 147
sprains 128
stain-removing products 41, 52-3
'Stay' command and gesture 18-20,
    18, 21, 33
stealing food **39**, *39*, 106
stings see accidents
stolen dogs **77**, *77*
stones, swallowing or chewing **75, 82**,
    82, 103
straining to pass urine **124**
stress 122
stroke (ailment) 150
submissive behaviour, excessive 26,
    34, 38, 48, *124*, 141
    building confidence 34
suntan cream 54
swelling see lump or swelling
swelling between toes see interdigital
    cysts
swellings or lumps in bitches **142**,
    142
swimming 146
    refusal to swim **75**, *75*
systematic desensitization see
    behaviour modification techniques

T

tablets, refusal to take **64,** *64*
tags see warts and papillomas
tattoo identification 78, 146
teeth 82, *82*, 114, 130-1, *130-1 see
    also* bad breath
    bones and 131
    broken teeth 130
    crooked teeth 130
    decay 131
    hard deposits on (calculus) 130
    retained milk teeth 130
    scaling 131
    tartar deposits (periodontal disease)
    131
    salt and baking soda 131
    toothpaste and brushes 131, *131*
teaching aids 22-3
terriers 76
territorial marking 12, 30, **56**, *56*, 124,
    138, 140
testicular neoplasia 97
testicular tumours 139
theobromine see chocolate
thyroid malfunction 108, 116, 136
ticks see fleas etc.
'tied' position in mating 85, *85*
toes, swelling between 133 *see also*
    limping
tonsillitis 120
tourniquet 135
toxaemia 108, 125
toy breeds 123
toys 29, 36, 39, 49, 59-60, 62, 76,
    82-3, 86, 97, 98, 103
training classes 20, 24
training discs 23, 25, *25*, 31, 34
travel sickness see car sickness
Tubigauze 134-5
tug of war see games
twitching see fits

U

underdog 31
urethra, inflammation of 124
urethral tumours 124
urinary tenesmus 124

urinating on lawn **84**
urinating on shrubs **74-5**, *74*
urination on command 18, 21, 55 *see also* house-training; puppies, house-training; soiling in house
urine
  bitch passing blood-stained and smelly urine **141**, *141*, 142
  bitch passing more frequently **140**
  blood in urine **125**
  not passing urine **124**
  straining to pass urine **124**
urolithiasis *see* bladder stones
urticaria (itchy wheals on skin) 133

V

vaccination 59, 91, 94, 146, 150
vacuum cleaners 57
vaginal discharge **143**
vaginal hyperplasia 141-2, 144
vaginal polyps 142
vaginal prolpase 142

vaginal tumours 124, 141, 143
vaginitis (inflammation of vagina) 140, 142-3
Vaseline 54, 58
Vet Bed 146
veterinary dentistry 130-1
veterinary surgeons and nurses 12, 25, 27-8, 30-1, 34, 42, 44-5, 49, 53-61, 63, 68-9, 70-1, *70*, 75, 77-8, 80-2, 90-105, 108-19, 121-47, *137, 139*, 150-3
vomiting **102-3**, *103*
viral infections 122
vitamin/mineral supplements 64
vulva, discharge from **126**
vulva, excessive licking of **142**

W

walks *see* exercise
warfarin poisoning 125
warts and papillomas 133
water on the brain (hydrocephalus) 132

water pistol *see* punishment
weakness and lethargy **136**, *136*
West Highland Terrier 68
whelping 99, 116, *122*, 125-6, 141, *141*, 143
worms and worming 60, 76-7, 100-1, 121, *121*, 126-7, 146 *see also* puppies
  roundworm (*Toxocara canis*) 76-7, 100-1, *101*
  tapeworm (*Dipylidium caninum*) 76, 100-1
  worm tablets 100
whistle, use in training 18, 41, 55
wounds, cuts and grazes 42, 63, 80-1, 114, **134-5**, *134*, 136
  in pads 135
  on ear flaps 135
wrist (carpus) 136

PICTURE CREDITS

Unless otherwise credited below, all the phototgraphs reproduced
in this book are from Interpet Publishing's own archive.
Bayer HealthCare (with thanks to Burak Borahan):
78 (both), 101 (top), 119 (top and middle).
Jane Burton, Warren Photographic: 15 (top right), 28, 59, 61,
70, 79, 80, 82, 85 (both), 88-9, 104, 108 (top), 112, 121, 124 (dog),
128, 141, 142, 143, 144-5.
Hills Pet Nutrition (with thanks to Emma Calder): 96 (uroliths), 125.
Merial Animal Health Ltd (with thanks to Rebecca Stevenson):
101 (lower), 117 (top right), 117 (bottom left), 119 (bottom).